What Wifey Won't Do My Sidepiece Will

RICHELLE T.

What Wifey Won't Do My Sidepiece Will

Copyright © 2021 Richelle T.

All rights reserved.

What Wifey Won't Do My Sidepiece Will is a work of fiction. Any resemblance to actual events, locations, or persons living or dead is coincidental. No part of this book may be reproduced in any written, electronic, recording, or photocopying form without written permission of the author, Richelle T.

Books may be purchased in quantity and/or special sales by contacting the publisher, Richelle T., by email at lataraphilips8@gmail.com.

Editing and Formatting: Tanisha Stewart
tanishastewart.author@gmail.com

Cover Design: Pat Sparks 3555
designedits@gmail.com

First Edition

Published in the United States
by Richelle T

Table of Contents

Chapter 1 1
Chapter 2 8
Chapter 3 11
Chapter 4 16
Chapter 5 22
Chapter 6 27
Chapter 7 31
Chapter 8 37
Chapter 9 43
Chapter 10 48
Chapter 11 54
Chapter 12 59
Chapter 13 63
Chapter 14 68
Chapter 15 74
Chapter 16 79
Chapter 17 84
Chapter 18 91
Chapter 19 99
Chapter 20 105
Chapter 21 113
Chapter 22 119
Chapter 23 125
Chapter 24 133

Chapter 25 141
Chapter 26 147
Chapter 27 153
Chapter 28 160
Chapter 29 170
Chapter 30 178
Chapter 31 187
Chapter 32 195
Chapter 33 200

What Wifey Won't Do My Sidepiece Will

Chapter 1

Rene

I stood outside Elizabeth's door, knocking repeatedly.
"Okay! I'm coming." Elizabeth opened the door. Once we were face to face, she smiled. "Oh, hello Rene." Elizabeth's tone was calm and collected.
"Where is he?" I asked, feeling ready for whatever. I looked past Elizabeth, trying to see if I could spot who I was looking for.
"Where is who?"
"Bitch, don't get snatched the fuck up. You know who. Where is Sam? I know he's here."
"Rene, I'm sorry, but Sam isn't here. I haven't seen him."
Does this bitch think I'm stupid? I thought to myself.
"Elizabeth, if I find out that you are trying to steal my husband, I will fuck you up and have your daughter calling me mommy. Trust me, I will take you down. Don't fuck with me, bitch."
"Damn, just calm down. It ain't that serious." Elizabeth was backing down from her previous sense of cockiness.
"I don't know how you figure that," I shot back, shaking my head. "You gotta be kidding me. You're laying up with my husband and got the nerve to say it ain't that serious. Bitch, don't test my gangster. I'm going to ask one more time, so you better listen good. Where is my goddamn husband?" I yelled.

"Alright, chill out. He was here earlier, but he had to leave."

"I knew his ass was here." Angry tears filled my eyes.

"Rene, please." Elizabeth looked like she felt for me. "I don't want you thinking I'm this bad woman who wants to steal your husband. Seeing him isn't as intentional as you may think. I'm not an evil person; trust me."

"Elizabeth, I don't trust anything that comes out of your mouth. Stay away from my husband. You no good ass bitch!" I slammed the door on my way out.

Once in the car, I couldn't hold it in any longer.

Tears began to fall from my eyes, as I sobbed in the privacy of my own space. The thoughts of Sam cheating on me hurt like hell. After all these years trying to love him, I couldn't believe that this was how he repaid me.

"Ungrateful son of a bitch!" I yelled out while hitting the steering wheel. I felt lost and alone. I needed to figure out my next move. "Oh boy... do I really want to go home or not? Jesus, what have I done to deserve this?"

After riding around for an hour, with no particular place in mind to go to, I decided to take it back home. As I parked in the driveway, I sat, dreading the thought of walking into the house. "I'm not up for this shit, but what the hell? I gotta face his lying, cheating ass eventually." I got out of the car.

Once in the house, Sam was on standby like he couldn't wait to confront me.

"Where in the world have you been?"

I stared at him, suspecting his guilt. I decided to play on his intelligence, since he was playing on mine.

I sighed. "Sam, I don't understand you. One minute, you're acting like you're a man trying to change, and the next minute you're on some bullshit, still seeing that hoe!"

"I'm not in the mood for this shit," he griped, with an angry shake of the head.

"I know you ain't! You've been spending time with that hoe just today."

"That's a lie."

"No, you're a lie! You know what? I'm getting sick of her ass calling and texting you, too." I jumped in Sam's face. "She says how high, and your stupid ass jumps? But see, I'm not stupid or blind. I know that piece of trash wants you. Deep down inside, you probably want her too."

I looked at Sam with my arms folded across my chest while waiting for his reaction. "Do you want Elizabeth or not?"

Sam continued his bullshit. "Rene, I don't know what has gotten into you lately, or where all of this is coming from, but I don't like it at all! To answer your question, no, I don't want Elizabeth. What do you want from me, Rene? Because I don't know; tell me dammit!"

I felt my blood pressure rising. My attitude was about to take a turn for the worst. "I want you to cut all communication from Elizabeth. I want you to pay more attention to our marriage and son. Leave that bitch alone. Spend more time looking for a job and bring some money into this house. Ever since you retired from the military, you just sit on your ass all damn day and watch sports and probably talk to her. Shit, you need to help cook, clean, do laundry, and take the trash out. Not only am I going to school, hell, I gotta work too."

"What are you talking about? Rene, you shouldn't be acting like this. I've been in the military for thirty years. I thought you would be happy having me home for a while. I guess I was wrong. Look, all I'm doing is trying to help Elizabeth fix up her house. Nothing is going on. You don't have to worry about me cheating."

"Really Sam? You said that once before and guess what you did? You fucking cheated on me! I have forgiven you once; not again." I could feel myself heating up even more.

"Alright Rene, shit," Sam cut in. "I did get me a piece of pussy on the side, but that was years ago. I have been faithful to you since then, though. Why are you coming at me hard like this? For what reason? Go ahead and say it. You still don't trust me; do you, Rene?"

"What the hell do you think? Hell no, I don't trust you."

"Rene, come here baby. I'm sorry." Sam looked at me with puppy dog eyes. "I know I have messed up in the past and I've been trying to make it up to you. That's why I retired from the military. To be home with you and Junior. Am I wrong about that?"

I sighed and unfolded my arms. "Where there is no trust, there is no marriage. I honestly thought having you here would make me happy."

"Wait, what are you saying? You want a divorce?" Sam was clearly not ready to give up on the marriage. "Rene, you mean the world to me."

"Sam, will you let me finish?"

"Go ahead."

"You spend so much time at Elizabeth's house that you don't do anything around here. You spend more time with her child than you do our son. No, I'm not trying to pick and choose your friends. However, if you are determined to make our marriage work, that means more time with your wife and son. And no more time with Elizabeth and Leah. I meant what I said: no more communication with them."

What Sam didn't know was that I had come home packing, with a blade hidden in my pants pocket. Before he realized it, I had taken the knife out and quickly pressed it against his neck.

"What the hell, Rene!" he let out in shock.

"See how I got you screaming out like a lil bitch? Just imagine what else I'll have you doing if you keep fucking with me."

"Rene."

"Just shut up and listen to me, Samuel Jacob Smith." The veins in my neck bulged, I was so mad. "If I find that you stepped outside this marriage again, I will kill you. I will break every bone in your damn body. Do you understand what I just said to you?"

"Rene, please lower the blade. I don't want no trouble with you. And yes, I heard you loud and clear."

"Do you now, Sam?" I pressed the knife a little deeper for emphasis. Not deep enough to cut him, but deep enough for him to catch my drift.

Our son, Junior, appeared in the kitchen doorway. "What's going on?" he asked, rubbing his sleepy eyes.

"Nothing; you okay?" I asked as I quickly put the knife down to my side and Sam stepped away from me, his eyes still on my weapon.

"What are you doing up?" I asked.

"I got thirsty," Junior said.

"Okay, you can have some juice then go back to bed."

"Yeah son," Sam said to Junior. He followed Junior into the kitchen. I reasoned he was doing that to get away from me and the knife I was still holding. "Alright, you've drank your juice; I will take you to your room and tuck you in."

I entered the kitchen, the knife safely back where I originally had it. I looked over at Sam. He was probably thinking about having to cut Elizabeth's ass off. I was sure he didn't want to because he definitely fucking her. He tried to act like he wasn't, but he was. *She's just a good friend's my ass; ain't no damn friend that good for him to neglect his wife and son.*

"Goodnight son," Sam said.

"Goodnight dad," Junior replied, but Sam did as he said he would and walked Junior back to his room to tuck him in for the night.

Meanwhile, in the kitchen, I had thoughts running through my mind like crazy. "He will not get away with this again. I let him slide once, even though it took me almost a year to forgive him and save our marriage. But he's not getting away with this shit anymore." Truth be told, I really wanted out of this marriage then. It took our son to reunite us as a family. I worked so hard to try to forget about Sam's cheating ways. The more I began to think, the more shit resurfaced, as my mind went back to the first time Sam had cheated.

It was a redheaded bitch named Rachel that came along and damn near destroyed our happy home. It took me forever to get Rachel's ass away from us. The crazy thing was that Rachel and Sam were in a relationship a year before I came along.

The ratchet bitch honestly thought I stole Sam from her.

Lies! I was getting out of my own relationship when Sam approached me at Delta's Café. I had no idea he was involved with anyone.

Apparently, I was a hard act to follow and it took Sam seven months just to get my number. Sam had swag, charisma, charm, and he carried himself as if he was a true royal prince. We always hung out together in public places, and we did everything together.

For the first five years, we were inseparable and couldn't get enough of each other. During his final week in the military, he dreaded the idea of going back across the seas. Hell, I did too. But I was determined to make most of me and Sam's time together. From there, we had dinner dates, including at my favorite restaurant in Charleston. It was magical affair.

I could remember the time when Sam was wearing a dark blue suit, a white shirt, a blue striped tie, and black suede shoes. Of course, I would match his swag with swag. I wore a long spaghetti dark blue dress, black heels with diamond earrings and a necklace to match. My hair was long and curly just how he liked it. I wore flawless makeup as well. I'd decided to get my nails and feet done the day before.

We were good for a long time after we starting dating. I could remember that special day just like it was yesterday. Sam had his fade tight, goatee trimmed and lined up. He was looking good as he came in asked me to take a long drive with him. Next thing I knew, we were pulling up Lakeshore Drive, where we could see the lights. I would never forget how Sam looked me in the eyes, and then gave me a long, passionate kiss.

He walked around and helped me get out of the car as we gazed at the beautiful sights before us. Sam got down on one knee with a two karat, gold diamond ring and asked for my hand in marriage. It took me forever just to get the word "YES!" out... I couldn't believe it. Every time I think about that day, it brings tears to my eyes. It took place on my birthday.

"God, what happened to us?" I whispered.

Chapter 2

Sam

"Goodnight son," I said to Junior. "Goodnight dad," Junior replied. As I watched my son close his eyes, I turned off his lamp and tiptoed out of the room. It took a long time to get Junior to trust me again after it was revealed during one of me and Rene's arguments years back that I'd previously cheated. I didn't want to hurt him after I hurt his mother, and yet I did it again. I hoped Elizabeth didn't catch feelings. For me, it was only sex. I really did love Rene with all my heart and soul; but truth be told, I wasn't ready to cash in my player's card yet.

Rene was the mother of my son. She was smart, beautiful, charming and strong minded. I could not stand when she became insecure about our marriage. Who was I kidding? I made her that way. Lord knows I didn't mean to. I decided right then that if it meant cutting off all communication with Elizabeth, I had no choice.

"Rene, where are you?" I slowly walked into the living room, where I saw Rene twirling her wedding rings. I could tell she was in deep thought so she didn't hear me when I called her name or walked into the living room. My heart dropped once I saw tears falling down her beautiful creamy chocolate face. I sat down beside her, wondering if she was going to look up at me. God, I loved my wife but I missed being single.

I leaned over, trying to pull Rene close to me and she tensed up. I didn't want to push the issue. I respected the fact she was mad as hell and hurt. I reached into my pockets and handed her a tissue. She accepted it.

"Honey, can I please talk to you? I want to work this out." She turned around to face me.

"Sam, I haven't forgotten about that phone call you were supposed to make to that bitch Elizabeth. Before we can talk, I suggest you make the call. Hit the speaker button and tell her that it is over. Right now!"

Of all the years I had known Rene, I'd never seen her ball her hands into a fist like she was ready to swing at me.

"Rene Denise Smith, I think you should calm down and lower your voice. Our son is upstairs sleeping."

"I will, once you make that phone call."

"Okay. I will call her now so we can sit and talk." I made sure I spoke in a calm manner. I reached into my pocket and took out my cell phone to dial Elizabeth's number. After several rings, she finally answered. "Hey Sam baby. How are you, sweet thang?"

"Uh, Elizabeth please don't call me sweet thang or baby. I'm calling to tell you that our friendship is over. I don't want you to contact me or my family again. You need to move on."

"Wait, hold on. Where is this coming from, Sam? Is it because of Rene? She can't control you or tell you who you can or can't be friends with. I'm not going to accept it. My daughter loves you and so do I."

On the inside, I wanted to yell, *What in the hell! It was only sex. I just used you. I got a wife and family.* Damn, I hoped this bitch wasn't pregnant. The last thing I needed was to have a child outside my marriage. *Damn it, Sam.*

"Elizabeth, I meant what I said. Have a nice life."

As I hung up, I turned to Rene. "Okay, Rene. You heard me tell her I don't want her contacting me or us."

She smacked me across my face in response.

Rene was 5'9 and 225lbs. She could be sweet as pie, but mean as a pit bull if you got on her bad side.

"Rene!" I rubbed the right side of my face.

"You slept with her, didn't you? Don't lie to me, Sam. It will only make things worse between us. I can't take no more of your cheating ways."

I saw how upset my wife was. I figured if I told her the truth, she would divorce me and take my son and I would never get them back. I did what I thought any man would do in my situation. I lied my ass off. "No baby we didn't have sex." I was trying so hard to sound convincing, but I knew Rene wasn't buying it. She gave me a cold stare, then her next words surprised me.

"Sam, for some reason I'm going to trust your word."

You could have knocked me over with a feather when I heard that. My face no longer hurt. I felt my nerves relaxing a little.

Rene continued, however, to make her point clear. "But if I find out anything different, I'm going to introduce you to a side of me that you never thought you would see in a million years. Do I make myself clear?"

I gulped. "Yes. No woman is worth me losing my family for. Once Rene's lip stuck out and her cat face appeared, I knew that meant she was going to watch me like a hawk. "I love you, beautiful."

Chapter 3

Rene

I don't know why Sam thinks I'm a fool. I'm a woman, not some side chick with no brain. Hell, I played this game with Sam way too long. I can forgive but I can't forget that he cheated on me before we got married, the whole time I was pregnant, and while he was overseas. All I've known him for is cheating. For now, I had stay calm and get some proof that Sam hadn't changed at all. Because now I was going to do the same thing to Elizabeth that I had done to Rachel.

"Sam, its late. I really don't feel like talking about this tonight. All I want is to take a bath and relax. Maybe get my thoughts together so I will know how we are going to deal with this issue. I'm hungry; I have not had anything to eat all day."

Hopefully that would buy me some time away from him, because I really needed to make a major phone call. To the one person who has always loved me, no matter what.

"Okay, beautiful, what can I do to help make you feel better?"

"Can you go to Oklahoma Styles Barbecue and get me some food or grab me a burger and tater tots from Sonic? I just want something to eat. I don't care what it is."

"Yes, I can do that. I'm going to grab my wallet and I will get us both a late-night dinner."

"Thank you." I gave Sam a quick kiss on the cheek. "Love you, baby."

When I saw Sam light up like a Christmas tree, I knew I had him hooked. Once I heard him get into his car, I knew my time was limited so I grabbed my cell phone and keys and went to sit in my car.

I dialed my favorite uncle's number. Billy "Dollar Bill" Marshall. After the second ring, he answered. Thank God, he was still up. "Hello," he said, in his sweet voice; low, but deep.

"Hi Uncle, how are you?"

"Well, hello honey!"

He was the only person I let call me honey. Every time he did, it always made me feel so special.

"Uncle, I don't feel so good. Could you come and spend time with me please." I tried not to cry, but he was the only one who understood me. We always had a special connection.

"Honey, talk to your uncle. What did that son of a bitch do now?"

"I don't have much time to talk, but I think Sam is cheating on me again. Uncle, please help me."

"Calm down; you know your uncle Billy got you. Tell me what you know."

"I know that he is spending too much time with this Elizabeth bitch and her daughter. He hasn't found no job to help keep the bills paid. Uncle I just don't know how much more I'm going to be able to take. I really do need you."

There was silence on the other end.

Hello? Uncle Billy, are you there?"

"Yes, honey. I'm still listening to every word you are saying. Listen to your old uncle. Do not get stressed out. I will take care of everything."

"Can you come tonight?"

Once I heard him giggle, that meant he was already getting a plan in mind to help me. "Let me find out what my schedule is, and I will let you know, okay honey?"

"Okay, love you."

"Love you more. Bye."

As we both hung up, I felt better knowing my uncle once again was going to help me get over my wife's intuition.

Sam

As I looked down at my phone, I saw that Elizabeth was calling me. She had already called me several times, but I was not going to answer her.

I need to find a way to fix our marriage before Rene called her uncle Billy "Dollar Bill" Marshall. He was no joke when it came to his nieces. You messed with Rene, it would be hell to pay. I found that out the hard way before.

When I cheated on Rene the first time, to this day, I still didn't know how Billy found out. I was overseas when it happened. All I knew was that when he came to see me, he took one look at me, and before I could stand up, he had a gun pointed at my face. He called me every name you could think of.

After my shift, me and a few other guys decided to go hang out. There he was again. This time, he came over to me and said, "Listen boy: when I give a direct order, I expect for you to be obey. Do you understand me? Let's go take a walk outside."

Like a dummy, I walked with him. I was 55 years old and he was 63, but I still had to give him my respect no matter what. When we reached a dark alley, I barely could see. All I felt was the bullet that had hit me in my chest.

God must have had mercy on my soul, because when I woke up, I was in the hospital. I had been there for six months.

My wife Rene was right there by my side, holding my hand. I decided to stay in the military for a few more weeks, then it was time for me to retire. I always did an awesome job saving my money over the years. I focused on the fact that I needed to be home with my wife and son when I retired. Rene kept urging me to get a job and not have us rely on my savings to pay the bills, but I was stubborn. I refused to work a regular nine to five when I had served in the military for most of my adult life. Finally, Rene got sick of me and started working part time jobs to keep money flowing. Everything was cool, from my perspective... until I came home to find Elizabeth sitting in my kitchen. That was when the temptation kicked in.

Rene had introduced us then went to college to get herself a better job since Junior was older. She rarely made time for Elizabeth and Leah, although she made time to be a mom and wife. I knew my wife was no fool. She knew me better than I knew myself.

I had to find a way to keep Rene from finding out this secret. This one I would take to my grave. Elizabeth could not ruin this for me. I would not let that happen because if Billy found out what I did, this time he would kill me for sure. I knew he wanted to last time when we crossed paths. This time, he would finish the job.

I married his favorite niece. Our son would lose all respect for me. There was nothing I could do about this. I had to protect them.

Damn, I wished I never met Elizabeth Waters.

Ring! I sucked my teeth and answered.

"Hello, Sam baby?" I heard Elizabeth's voice.

"What do you want, Elizabeth? I told you that I don't want to talk to you anymore. Now stop calling me and having feelings for me."

"Why are you denying me? What we have is real and special!"

"It's not! Elizabeth I gotta go. My wife isn't the type you want to play games with. This is not a joke Elizabeth. I mean it; leave me the hell alone. Don't you ever call me again."

Hanging up in her face, I hoped she took me seriously. Billy "Dollar Bill" Marshall and his stepbrother, Kingston Marshall, would have me in a casket before I could take Martin Lawrence's Thanksgiving advice: "Pass the peas like we used to do."

Chapter 4

Elizabeth

"I can't believe he hung up on me. Doesn't he know I meant what I said?" Elizabeth yelled. "I really do love Samuel. So does Leah. I know that we were meant to be together."

Elizabeth sat in her emotions, alone at her kitchen table. "I had that feeling the moment when we first laid eyes on each other." She sat at her table, talking to herself since no one wanted to answer her calls. "I felt a spark rush through my body when we shook hands. After Rene had introduced us, I didn't want to let go. I just wanted to give him the best thrill sex he ever had." Elizabeth cried into her hands. When she calmed herself, she continued.

"I remember the first night he was sitting outside smoking a cigarette. I stepped outside to enjoy my e-cigarette. I would watch him put that cigarette up to his lips thinking to myself, *I wish that was me."* Elizabeth looked at her phone again, willing it to ring with a call from Sam. It didn't. She continued her story.

"I said to myself, what the hell? Go on and talk to him. I had finally worked up the courage to say hi..."

"Oh, hi Elizabeth," Sam had said.

"I wanted to bust a nut after he said my name." Elizabeth cackled at the memory.

"What are you doing up so late?" Sam asked.

"Leah is sleeping. I'm trying to stop smoking, but it doesn't look like I'm going to anytime soon. What about you?"

"I just came out to smoke and enjoy a peaceful night. It's been a long time since I enjoyed the stars and moon."

When Sam said that, he gave Elizabeth a suggestive look. She wasn't sure though. His next words confirmed her suspicions. "Plus, I just made passionate love to my wife. So now she is sleeping."

"Yeah, I heard you two really going at it." Elizabeth gave Sam a suggestive look of her own, but she was still unsure.

"I could tell for a split moment that Sam was a little embarrassed by my comment." She smirked.

"Oh, I'm sorry we were that loud," Sam apologized.

"Truth be told, I could have made him scream like that; even louder. Sam and I had been talking for a few weeks. I was really enjoying his company more than Rene's. Rene was always busy with school and work. I knew Sam didn't have a job, with Rene always nagging at him to get one. I noticed how much Sam was getting stressed. A fine man like him didn't need that. One morning, I saw Rene leaving. I knew how much Sam loved his morning coffee and breakfast."

Elizabeth hugged herself as she continued.

"I knocked on their back door since I'd already seen Junior leave for school. Leah was with her so-called daddy. I invited Sam over. We shared nice cup of coffee then breakfast."

Elizabeth blushed as she remembered that day.

"That's when I knew it was now or never. I made sure I was gentle, but firm as I pressed against his manhood. He realized how much I wanted to feel him inside of me.

I asked him, just to be sure: If I secretly gave you a gift, would you take it?"

Sam smiled as if he wasn't sure what gift I was referring to.

"What kind of a gift?" he'd asked.

"Close your eyes," I had demanded, full of boldness now.

"I pulled down his sweatpants and boxer shorts and slowly opened my mouth."

Elizabeth smirked.

"I could tell he was enjoying it cause once I felt him grab a handful of my hair and moan. I knew I had to make him mine."

"Oh, Elizabeth! Damn, I'm about to cum. You got to stop it," Sam pleaded.

"I just ignored him and kept on sucking. I wanted him to cum in my mouth. I needed to taste his chocolate juices. Hell, what Rene won't give him I sure will!"

"Damn Elizabeth," Sam whispered.

"Oh, once I got a good taste of Sam's dick once again, I looked up and saw him smile. I finally released him... I got up from my knees and helped him pull back up his boxers and sweatpants."

"Well what did you think?" I asked.

"It was okay, but Rene got some damn good sex game. Thanks for a great morning. I got work to do around the house and errands to run before my wife and son get home."

Elizabeth's eyes blurred as she came back to the present.

"I just stood there in shock as he walked out the back door like it was nothing. Isn't that some shit for your ass." She spat on the floor.

"At first I started to get mad, then I felt a little smile coming on. I want Sam. I will stop at nothing to get him. Rene doesn't deserve him. I do, Samuel Jacob Smith. You belong to me and only me. We will be together; that I can promise you."

Elizabeth raised her glass of wine to an empty kitchen.

"Rene better enjoy her fun in the sun and time with you."

She took a sip, then slammed the glass down on the table. Thankfully, it wasn't fragile, or it would have broken.

"Oh, Sam! You are the only man I will forever want. Even if I have to get rid of Rene for you, then so be it!" Elizabeth screamed.

"I would dare that bitch to try and stop me. She honestly thinks moving you away will keep us apart? Well it won't."

Elizabeth pounded on the table with her next words. "I will not go down without a fight. Maybe I should fake a pregnancy test. Pay someone to give me copies of their ultrasound pictures. Sam just can't come into our lives, then walk away from us.

Just because Rene isn't woman enough to share… I need a man in my life too. I'm tired of being a single mom. It's a full-time job since the state of Oklahoma took my other children from me. Leah is all I got. Yeah, she's all I got."

Elizabeth's eyes were getting droopy. She needed to take her meds soon. Fuck those meds though. She wasn't crazy.

Elizabeth stared into space as unpleasant memories filled her mind. Specifically, the money that was on her head for double-crossing her previous friends. She tried not to think of bad things for too long though. Her mind preferred to consume itself with Sam.

"Ever since then, I've been secretly after him." A wicked smile grew across her features. "I am the one he needs; not her. Rene is too damn controlling. Always suspicious of my friendship with him. I need to come up with a plan for how I could end their marriage. It most certainly wouldn't be the first time I broke up a happy home."

Elizabeth smirked.

"That's how Leah was born. I was friends with Becky, then Matt came along. I first met Becky in a shelter. Matt was one of the cooks. He and Becky started talking a few months, then a friendship had developed. After two years of friendship, they began to date. That following year, they were married.

I met Jeff, who was an abusive asshole. I cried on Becky shoulders. She told me to move in with them. I felt like the third wheel. Watching those two love birds made me sick. Becky got a job as a housekeeper, which was funny to me; she barely cleaned her own home. I kept it cleaned most of the time."

Elizabeth raised the glass up to her lips again to take another sip, then she realized it was empty. She put the glass back down.

"Matt came down with the flu. I became his nurse. While Becky was working and making money, I was making a secret family. I kept Matt dosed up with medicine and painkillers. While he was unconscious, I was on top of him fucking his brains out, sucking his dick hard and fast as I could before the meds wore off. A month later, I found out that I was pregnant. Once Matt was feeling a lot better, I tried my hardest to hide my baby bump as the next few months went by. Leah came early. When Leah was getting older, she started to look just like Matt with brown hair and blue eyes. Becky knew who Leah's biological father was. She knew Matt had gotten me pregnant. Matt kept denying we had sex. There was no way he could have sex with me; he was out with the flu.

Becky challenged him to a DNA test, and eight weeks later the results showed Matt was the father. Becky and Matt threw me and Leah out.

Becky had said to her husband, "Either it's the bitch's child or your wife?" He chose to keep Becky. I filed for child support, but what the hell is twenty-five dollars a month is going to do? I never thought I would have a desire for another man again until I had met Sam.

Now I need to remove Rene from Sam's life but how will I do it without getting caught?"

Elizabeth finally fell silent as she developed another plan.

Chapter 5

Rene

Sitting in my car listening to my favorite uncle Billy calm my nerves, I realized that I didn't want to lose my husband to some fat nasty woman who took pleasure in breaking up happy homes and destroying families. All I knew was that any time Elizabeth wanted to fight, I would give her the beating of a lifetime.

I couldn't wait to see my uncle Billy. It had been so long since we spent any family time together. I would prepare his favorite meals. Just thinking about it brought a smile to my face. I knew I didn't have much time. Sam would be home any minute now.

"Uncle Billy, I appreciate you taking the time out to spend with me. I will be fine. If you want, you can bring Uncle Kingston. I haven't seen him since he was released from prison. It would be nice to have my family come out."

"Yes, I know honey. But I still say you really need to keep a close eye on Sam's sneaky ass and that bitch as well. Just don't let her anger cloud your better judgement," Billy explained.

"I will try. It's just so hard for me right now. I want to tear her head off so bad. You have no idea how angry and hurt I am feeling. This was not supposed to be this way."

"Honey, yes I do know the feeling all too well. Just remember who taught and trained you."

"Yes, Uncle. I will never forget where I come from or what I stand for. Look, thanks for the talk. I know that Sam will be on his way home soon. I can handle my own problems. I just needed my favorite uncle to help me get through this."

"Your uncle is always here whenever you need me." Billy smiled.

"Thanks for listening. I can't wait for you to come out and visit me."

"I'll be there."

"Goodnight, Uncle Billy. I will see you soon."

"Goodnight love."

I hung up the phone. I knew my favorite Uncle Billy like the back of my hand. He was going to get in touch with Kingston to form a plan. Until I could figure out what the plan was, I would just have to play this one by ear.

Billy

After hanging up with Rene, Billy decided to reach out to Kingston. He needed his brother to form a plan. Sam was back to his old tricks again. This was just like the time he had cheated on Rene with Rachel's hoe ass.

Now he was starting it again. The question was why? Billy and Kingston would be spending a lot of time in good old Colorado. He needed a vacation.

Going through his contacts on his phone for Kingston, Billy knew that he would still be up. Kingston could sometimes turn himself into a vampire, as he loved to describe himself. Kingston answered on the third ring.

"Hello."

"Hello," Billy said. "Brother, we got a problem that needs to be solved in Colorado immediately."

Kingston perked up at that. "Then I need to know what kind of a problem I can help solve."

"It's Rene. Sam is up to his old tricks again."

"Dammit! Didn't we solve that problem years ago? Why don't she just file for a divorce and leave that sorry ass bastard alone."

"You know Rene loves him, but she just needs her family. She got a feeling that Sam is having an affair again. She mentioned a lady named Elizabeth."

"I still don't see the problem. Do we have evidence to indicate that Sam is still up to his old tricks?"

"No brother, we don't have any proof that he is, but this case needs to be handled secretly. Rene can't know anything about it. I can't afford to have her upset about my plan to get rid of Sam and whoever this Elizabeth lady is. I want his ass erased from my precious niece's life. I understand they share a child, but it's no excuse to keep on mistreating them the way he does." Billy was yelling now; he was so mad.

"Calm down brother. Anything that you need, you know that I am always here. Just remember that Rene is my niece too. I love her and Junior just as much as you do."

"Once again, you are correct brother. As always."

Kingston smiled, knowing Billy really wanted Sam dead. Being the half-brother of a drug lord, if Billy had it his way, he would have killed Sam years ago. Kingston also knew how much Rene loved Sam.

"Are you coming or not, brother"? Billy asked.

"I wouldn't miss it for the world. Go to bed and get some rest. Rene knows what she is doing. She has been trained by the best there is," Kingston reassured his brother.

"I know, but if that bastard hurts my baby just once more, I will have no choice but to erase him forever."

Kingston laughed. He knew how Billy felt. He had felt the same way about Tiana. Nobody messed with those two ladies and lived to talk about it.

"Yeah, I will soon. I'm guessing you are still torturing Jaxson's sorry ass." Billy laughed, already knowing the answer to the question.

"Yeah, I am loving every minute of it. He can't see me, but I can see him. Tiana knows where I am. She will never tell anyone about me or my whereabouts." Kingston loved having a secret place that he could call his own. He loved living with Tiana and her son.

"Brother, why don't you show yourself to the family?"

Kingston growled his response. "I don't want to see those sons of bitches! Especially that bitch Virginia."

Billy knew ever since Kingston's mother, LillyMae, had passed, Kingston felt a part of his heart and life died with her. Billy wished he could have gotten to know LillyMae. All of the stories that Kingston would tell him about her, he felt he knew her. Thank God for Tiana, who kept Kingston going and wrapped around her little finger.

"I understand brother. Just remember: Rene is going to need us a lot more than she realizes."

"Yeah, I know. Well, we both best to get to bed. Tell Tiana I said hi and I can't wait to meet her."

"No problem, brother."

Kingston

Disconnecting the call from Billy, Kingston couldn't leave Tiana in Tulsa all by herself. He needed his baby girl with him now that she was all grown up, living on her own.

    Kingston had an extra key to her house and he could go over there anytime he wanted to. Tiana was always happy to see him. They shared a close relationship.

    He needed to go check on his baby girl. He knew she had been dating some guy, but she refused to tell him who. Not only was he enjoying slowly getting his revenge on his brother Jaxson, he needed to find out who this guy was that was dating his baby. He needed to let him know the rules.

Chapter 6

Billy

Billy couldn't sleep without placing a call to Sam. He'd be damned if Sam hurt his family again. Sam needed to be reminded not to get caught slipping.

Picking up the cordless phone once more, Billy knew he should just wait. He dialed anyway.

"Hello," Sam answered.

"Do I need to remind you of the job I could have finished across the seas?"

Sam immediately knew what Billy was referring to. "No, you don't. I have no idea what this phone call is about."

"Let me just say this: you better pray every day, before I decide to send you to Jesus because can't you keeping your fucking pants on. I'll be damned if Rene suffers from one of your damn side bitch's pussies again. She may have saved your ass once. She will not save you again!"

"Hang on Billy. I know I've made some mistakes in the past; however, there is no need to threaten my life. I love Rene with all my heart and soul. I have no intentions of hurting her or our son ever again: I promise you that."

"This better be the one time you keep your damn promise. If I find out different, I promise you I will fucking kill you. Do not make me go there with you, boy."

Sam

I disconnected the call. I didn't want to continue to have this conversation with Billy or with Kingston. I knew they were double trouble. I needed to cover my tracks; maybe convince Rene or Elizabeth to leave town. I shouldn't have slept with Elizabeth in the first place. I just couldn't resist the temptation. I'd always wondered what it felt like to sleep with a white woman.

Now Kingston was calling, interrupting my train of thought.

"Hello," I answered.

"Listen negro, I better not ever find out that you are still up to your old damn tricks. I just had an interesting conversation with my brother. If my niece gets hurt by you one more time it will be your last time, and that is a promise that I will keep. No nigger is going to fuck over my babies. I will kill anyone who will tries to. I will feed you to the lions. It's not Billy you need to worry about; it's me."

"Listen Kingston; I am going to tell you the same thing that I just told your brother: I will never hurt Rene ever again. You got my word on it."

"Yeah right. For some reason, I don't trust your word. Billy might feel different, but I can't speak for him; I can only speak for me. I will be making a trip out there to see my family. I need to see solid proof that she is fine and doesn't need to be worried about this bitch named Elizabeth or whoever the fuck she is. All I know is that you better have covered your ass and tracks by the time we make an appearance. Right now, it would feel so good to break your damn jaw. You might have army training, but I got prison and street training. You have no idea how deadly or dangerous I can be. I don't like you: never have and never will. I don't trust the damn ground that you walk on. I don't fear you. But you will fear me from this day forward."

Kingston

Disconnecting the call, Kingston was so upset, he couldn't even think straight. First it was Jaxson, Virginia, Chyna and several others. Now he had to deal with Sam and his lies. He meant what he said: nobody messed with the people he loved. There were very few people that Kingston did love and trust. Looking at LillyMae's picture, Kingston wished he was home to take care of her. When she died, his world stopped.

Tiana was the closest to his heart from the day she was born. He was in love with her. Now that she had grown up, with a son of her own to raise, Kingston thought she couldn't handle it. To his surprise, Tiana turned out to be a wonderful mother. The only mystery was that she refused to tell him who the father was. Kingston would have added him to the list of people to track down.

Kingston would die for Tiana. He would also get his revenge on Jaxson; everyone kept telling him that Jaxson was free, and Tiana knew where he was.

Kingston was asleep in the guest bedroom when Virginia came over and starting yelling at Tiana, looking for him. To his surprise, Tiana held her own. She stood and defended his honor. He couldn't have been more proud of her. Kingston reasoned that Tiana sure had inherited her grandmother's attitude, just from listening to their argument.

Kingston started to get up and join them in the living room. He was going to give Virginia an ear full. With the way Tiana was handling it, however, he stayed put.

"Listen, you might be grown up, but you will show me some respect," Virginia explained.

Did you show my grandma respect when you stole all of her money?" Tiana responded. "Don't you dare come to my house and talk to me about respect. You no good bitch! Don't worry about where my uncle is; that is none of your business, or Jaxson's. If you loved and cared so much about him, you wouldn't treat him the way you do. Now get the fuck out my house before I really get disrespectful."

Virgina sniffed. Kingston imagined her standing there with her arms crossed, trying to hold an unbothered expression on her face. "Fine with me. I will find him. And if you knew what was good for you then you would keep your distance from him and that sweet little baby boy. There are things about him that you don't even know about."

"I know you better stop with this bullshit and leave."

Virginia

As Virginia was leaving, she knew that Tiana knew more than what she was telling. She would get to the bottom of this.

Chapter 7

Rene

I couldn't understand what was taking Sam so long to get back. Not that I really cared. I needed this time alone. Maybe I should take Junior and leave go on a vacation; just the two of us. I needed a drink but decided against it. It wouldn't solve my problems.

Continuing to look out the window up at the stars, I wished LillyMae was still alive. She always knew what to say. I questioned if I ever should have married Sam. I shook my head. Despite all of the hell he had put me through, I still loved him. But was this marriage worth fighting for?

Divorces could be hurtful and messy. I thought I had married the perfect man. How could I have been so blind? Finally, I saw Sam pulling into the driveway. I felt myself relax, quickly wiping away my tears. I didn't want him to see. Not that he hadn't seen them before, when he had his first affair. I remembered all the screaming, shouting, and yelling I had done back then. The next day, I went to file for divorce. I was so weak, I fainted in the lawyer's office. They had to call for an ambulance and rush me to the hospital. When I awakened, the first thing I saw was Sam with a big smile on his face.

"Why are you smiling at me, you son of a bitch! I want a divorce; I will not be treated this way."

Sam's smile quickly left his face. He didn't know I wanted to end the marriage. That was not why he was smiling though; he was overjoyed that we were having a baby. We were going to be a family. In a year or so, he could retire from the army and be home with his wife and child.

"Rene honey, I am sorry about what I did but I am smiling, or I was, until you sprung this news on me, because we are going to have a baby. I found the pregnancy test in the trash this morning. When I got the call that you were here, I rushed right over. They ran some tests and confirmed that we are going to be parents."

Damn it, I thought I hid that test before I left. *I was so mad and angry that I must not have done a very good job,* I thought to myself.

I refused to say a word to Sam. He tried to reach for my hand, but I snatched it away. Just as I was about to say something, Billy and Kingston came walking in with lots of gifts. I knew that I had to really put on a happy face before all hell broke loose.

"Hello, I didn't know that you guys were coming. How did you find out that I was here?" I forced a smile that probably looked more like a grimace.

They both smiled before answering my question.

"A little birdie told us," Kingston answered.

I couldn't take their excitement. I knew the little birdie had to be Sam. I wished he would have just left me alone. I also knew now wasn't the time. I was ready to go home and be with my family.

"How are you honey?" Kingston asked.

"Now Uncle, if you knew that Tiana heard you calling anyone that name beside her, she would have a fit. I am fine; I'm ready to go home and relax. I got so much work to do."

Kingston and Billy knew something was wrong and they both knew Sam was to blame for what happened to me and why I ended up in the hospital. They waited until the doctor came in to see why I was there.

The doctor came in with the test results.

"Hello, I am doctor Shelby Henderson and I have your test results back. Everything is fine except for one little detail."

"Well, get on with it. I want to know what is going on with my baby girl."

"Congratulations! You are having a baby," Dr. Shelby stated.

Kingston looked down at me and gave me a big hug, flashing his famous dimpled smile. What he didn't realize was that Dr. Shelby was checking him out. Billy gave me a hug next. He was glad to know it was nothing serious.

"I will leave you all alone to process the wonderful news, and Rene, I will be having you discharged. If you need me or have any questions or concerns, feel free to contact me."

"Thanks Doc; I will."

Sam

When we found out Rene was pregnant, I wanted to go over and hold my wife and apologize for hurting her the way I had. I made a promise that I would not cheat on her again. I was becoming a father, a role model. I needed to prepare for this unborn child. It was time for me to put away my childish behavior and step up to the plate.

"Well Sam, congrats on your big news," Kingston had chimed in when Dr. Shelby announced the news.

"Thanks Kingston. Now that we are going to be one big happy family, I will alert the base and let them know that I am going to be a dad. Pretty soon I am going to retire from the military. Rene and the baby need me at home with them."

"No! I will be fine without you. Go on and continued to serve your country. My uncles will take care of us," Rene had said.

Billy and Kingston knew for sure that something was not right with her. I knew they would have a talk with her later. After she was released from the hospital. Moments later, the nurse came in to give her the discharge papers. Rene looked like she couldn't have been happier.

After getting dressed, she looked at everyone with concern. My wife wasn't too good at hiding her true feelings.

Rene

When I found out about the pregnancy, I wished that Tiana came out to visit. At least I would have had another female in the house to talk to. We were more like sisters than cousins. I missed her. I planned to call her and give her the good news. Maybe she would come out to Colorado.

"Kingston, take Sam out of here. I want to have a chat with Rene for a minute," Billy had said.

Kingston looked at Sam, and they walked out quietly, closing the door behind them.

"Alright baby girl, I know you well enough to know when something is wrong. You don't seem thrilled about Sam's retirement, or the baby."

"You're right; I am not excited about it. I went to the lawyer's office to file for a divorce. Sam has been having an affair behind my back. I know I should be happy about the baby, but I'm not thinking about giving the baby up or just aborting it. As crazy as it may seem after I say it, I'm hoping to miscarry."

Billy

Billy was shocked. There were no way in hell he was going to let that happen. This was the second time that Sam had cheated on Rene, according to his knowledge. The first time he had no proof other than what Rene had suspected. He just followed her lead, which was a dead end. He knew that Sam was a no-good bastard. But he made it his mission to take Kingston across the seas and let Sam know that when it came to Rene, they would end his life.

Billy was curious: how did she find out that he was having an affair? He asked his niece, and her answer infuriated him even more.

"He told me. He could no longer keep it a secret or continue to lie to me, and he confessed the entire thing. It's a hard pill to swallow. This isn't the first time that he did this. He has been cheating on me throughout our entire relationship. I thought once we got married that he would stop. I guess I was wrong."

Rene had no idea that how badly Billy wanted to end Sam's life. To him, Rene had to be the strongest woman on earth. No other woman would have stayed as long as she did. Billy planned to talk to Kingston and let him know. There was no more talking to Sam; it was time they showed him that they meant business.

"Alright sweetheart; let's go get some food in your stomach. We got to feed my little baby. And you will keep this baby. That is my blood you are carrying. Sam night be a true asshole but the baby doesn't deserve to get punished. However, Sam does, and will."

Chapter 8

Kingston

Kingston and Sam had decided to walk down to the cafeteria to grab a cup of coffee. The more Kingston kept his eyes on Sam, the more he felt that he was guilty of something. He would talk to Billy about it. Rene always confided in Billy, just like Tiana always confided in him.

"Sam, why do you look so guilty? I sure hope that I don't have to remind you about what I would do to you if you have done anything to hurt my family."

Sam looked pissed. "Man damn, why do you always have to sweat me? Every time you guys come out to visit or talk to Rene, you keep coming at me like I am a punk bitch."

Kingston walked up to Sam and punched him in the stomach. Watching Sam double over in pain, Kingston picked him up and threw him against the wall. He landed another punch in his jaw.

"Now look here: that may be your wife, but that's my family and you will not try me again. You say you ain't a punk bitch, but you're acting like one. I didn't know that the military allowed punk bitches like you who can't swing back serve our country. What a fucking joke." Kingston laughed.

Rene

Uncle Billy continued to console me. "I'm sorry you had to face that by yourself. I will be honest with you: I can't believe you kept that from me. I always known that you two were having problems; I just didn't know to what extent."

"It's alright; it's not your fault. I really thought that I could handle it on my own without me always coming to you or Uncle Kingston. I needed to fight my own battles. I knew what I was getting into when I first got involved with Sam."

"I wish you never married him."

"I know; that's why I went to go file for a divorce, but Sam really wants to work things out. I don't want to be one of the women who says, "I only stayed for the sake of our child." And who knows? Maybe this baby will be a huge change for us. Every child deserves to have both parents in their lives." I said it, but I was still trying to make myself believe it.

I wasn't fooling Billy with my speech; I could tell. "Yes, they do, but they don't deserve to be used as pawns in their parents' bullshit, or grow up in an unhappy home."

We fell silent, and Billy helped me pack up my things. He was getting hungry. He couldn't think on an empty stomach. I was staring at my uncle. I hoped I didn't cause any sadness or grief or bring back horrible childhood memories. I was grateful to have Billy in my life. He took on the role of my dad, not my uncle. He treated me the same way that Kingston treated Tiana.

"I'm hungry and I know that you are too. I can hear your stomach growling." I laughed.

"Of course, I am hungry. I came all the way out here on an empty stomach." Billy smiled.

We decided to head to a nearby restaurant. On our way out, we spotted Kingston sitting in the waiting area reading a magazine. Sam apparently was gone. I looked around to see if I could spot him. After a few moments, I asked Kingston where he was.

"He is in the cafeteria. I will go get him."

Shelby

Dr. Shelby could feel butterflies in her stomach. She wanted to get to know her patient Rene's uncle, Kingston. Her other uncle, Billy, was good looking too, but he was no match for Kingston.

Shelby was going to have to talk to Rene to see if she could fill her in on her uncle. The young woman seemed friendly enough. Shelby hoped that she wasn't overstepping her bounds by asking, though in her heart she knew she clearly was. She just prayed that Kingston would come back and talk to her.

"Hey Rene, can I have a spare moment of your time?" Shelby asked.

Rene looked up at Shelby from her seat. "What's up?"

Shelby couldn't help but blush before asking, "I was wondering about your Uncle Kingston; does he have a special lady or children in his life?"

Rene

I wanted to burst out laughing, but I knew I would only embarrass Dr. Shelby. I assessed her and thought about how she had treated me during my brief stay at the hospital that day, and decided she was genuine.

"The only special lady that is in his life is Tiana, my cousin. Uncle Kingston doesn't have any children. Tiana is more of his daughter than niece. Look, if you want his number, just ask him. Or I could write it down and give it to you. Before I do, I will ask him. After that, you owe me big time." I smiled.

Shelby shot a smirk of her own. "You got a deal. Oh God; when He created Kingston, He showed out, didn't he girl? I just love a man who got swag and charm. Oh, and his voice. I could listen to him talk all day. Move over Barry White, there is a new sheriff in town." Shelby laughed.

"Dr. Shelby, Uncle Kingston has a low baritone voice that is sweet and soft. But if you think he sounds like Barry White, that will be our little secret."

I shook my head as we spotted Kingston and Sam walking toward us, until Kingston stopped Sam and the two had a secret conversation.

Sam

Kingston threatened me with his eyes. "Look, Sam. Rene doesn't need to know that we had a chat, or that I just roughed you up to prove my point. Understand?" Kingston spoke like he was ordering me.

I didn't say anything. I just wanted to get away from Kingston as far as I could. Kingston would not make me a punk bitch. I didn't let the other soldiers treat me that way. I kept walking without saying a word. Sooner or later, I would challenge him to a real fight. I'd be damned if I continued to put up with Kingston's disrespect.

Kingston

When Kingston got back over to where Rene was standing with her doctor, he saw that she was all smiles. She had that look of michief in her eyes. He wondered what that was about, but he didn't have to think for long. "Uncle Kingston," Rene began, "let me introduce you to Dr. Shelby Henderson. She would love if you two could exchange phone numbers. By the way, she loves your voice."

Shelby was trying to hide the red in her cheeks. It was too late; Kingston had already seen it. He smiled at the last comment that Rene said. Between her and Tiana, they were always trying to find him a woman. Kingston wasn't shy by any means; he just wasn't ready to settle down. Before he went to prison for thirty years, he fell in love with Rebecca.

Kingston thought Rebecca would always love him, but all she wanted was his money. LillyMae couldn't stand her. Kingston tried so hard to get LillyMae to change her mind about Rebecca and get to know her. After so many tries, he just gave up. LillyMae knew from the start that Rebecca was not wife material. She warned him that he should leave her alone.

Kingston was blinded by love. When he got caught for his crimes, he tried to reach out to Rebecca. She never showed up for any of his court dates or came to visit him, so he used his connections and found out that she moved to Texas.

A month into his sentencing, he had to beg LillyMae to track Rebecca down in Texas. When LillyMae gave in, she got Rebecca's contact information and gave it to him. It took him several days to call her. When he finally got the nerve, she was not happy at all that he found her. She called him every name but a child of God. From that moment on, Kingston refused to share his heart with any female except LillyMae and Tiana.

Shaking the thought from his mind, Kingston realized everyone was staring at him. They didn't know where he had zoned out to.

"Hey bro, you alright? It looks like you were in outer space." Billy asked with a concerned look on his face.

"Yes, I am fine. I just remembered to give Tiana a call. It's been too long since I spoke to her."

"Alright; let's get a move on. I'm hungry as a horse."

Billy

Sam and Kingston picked up the gifts that they had brought for Rene. Billy stayed behind to ask Rene about Shelby. He couldn't help but smile at her. Shelby returned his smile then went back to work.

"Hey Rene, did Shelby ask for my number? I could feel her sexy bedroom eyes watching my every move." Billy chuckled.

"Nope! She was watching Uncle Kingston and wanted his number. That's why I am writing it down, so she can call him. He gave me permission to give it to her. Better luck next time, Uncle Billy." Rene laughed.

"That's not funny. You know we could pass for twins. Are you sure that she didn't get us mixed up? Maybe she said Kingston, but was really referring to me."

"Uncle Billy, get over it. No, she didn't get you two mixed up. She wanted Uncle Kingston. There are plenty more fish in the sea. Now let's go," Rene ordered.

Rene

I saw Shelby and slipped her Kingston's number as I was leaving. We hugged and said our goodbyes.

"You know it was me and not Kingston," Billy said as we exited the building. "You really gave her my number for her to call me. It's cool; I will just pretend it was a surprise." He beamed.

"Uncle Billy, for the final time she wants Uncle Kingston, not you."

Chapter 9

Elizabeth

Elizabeth was pacing back and forth in her living room. There was no way in hell that she would lose to Rene. She had suffered and lost enough in her lifetime. She had to win; she had to get rid of her. The more Elizabeth thought about it, the more evil she was becoming. She wanted Sam so bad that she could taste him. She knew she wanted him the very first time she met him.

Even more when she surprised him and sucked his dick. She could suck his dick for hours every day and night. He tasted so good, swallowing every single drop of him.

Sam was meant for her, not Rene. Rene didn't appreciate a man like Sam, but Elizabeth did. She had to make him see that. They could be a blended family. Their children could be brother and sister. It wasn't fair that Rene got to be a wife and mother. All Elizabeth got to be was a single parent.

She already let one guy get away from her; she would not let Sam get away from her. Not by a long shot. She picked up the phone to call Sam again. She was craving his voice, his dick inside of her.

Sam

I felt my phone vibrate. Looking at the caller ID, I saw Elizabeth's name on the screen. I wasn't sure if I should answer, but I knew if I didn't, she would just keep calling back. After this, I would need to block her number. I couldn't lose my family. I had no choice but to get rid of Elizabeth. I made my bed and now I had to lay in it.

Many years ago, I did some research on Rene's family. I was no match for her two crazy uncles. I was amazed to find out that when Kingston was in prison, he had everyone at his feet. What he said went; no question about it. Even the warden bowed down to him. The reason was because Kingston could destroy his family.

Already getting annoyed by her constant calls, I started to regret the day I met Elizabeth. I prayed that she would stop calling me. After the first five times I saw her name flash across the screen, I decided I might as well get it over with.

"What! I thought I told you to get lost? I never want to see or hear from you again. Get that through your thick skull. I love my wife, Elizabeth. I wish that you would disappear. Move to another state and ruin somebody's else life."

"Oh Sam, you're so cute when you are wrong. I will never leave you. We belong together. You were meant for me, not Rene. She doesn't understand you like I do, nor will she give you what you need. I can give you that and more. We can be a family; a beautiful blended family."

I looked at my phone before putting it back to my ear. "Have you lost your damn mind? You need to stop watching that Kardashian show. I don't want you, never have and never will. Now leave me the hell alone before I will be forced to take action against you and you don't want that. Never contract me again. Stay away from my family. I mean it, Elizabeth."

I hung up in her face, hoping she would take me seriously. I really did love Rene and would do anything to keep my family together. I should have asked Billy and Kingston when they were planning to come out and visit. I needed time to cover my ass and keep Elizabeth at bay. Next time Rene got her hands on Elizabeth, she would be on life support fighting for her life.

I couldn't have my wife sitting in jail or serving time in prison for the crimes that I had committed. It wasn't fair to her or our precious son that we shared. I didn't realize how lucky I was until I made a huge mistake by sleeping with Elizabeth. Only God himself could save me from the heat I was about to face.

Rene

Why is he still parked in the driveway? From what I just witnessed, it seemed like Sam was yelling at someone. I was watching him through the window and hoping that he would decide to go back to the military.

He hadn't worked since he retired. I thought once he did that, things would be so much better. Boy was I wrong.

After thirty years of being a military wife, here I was, battling myself about filing for divorce. Of course, I didn't want Junior growing up in a single parent home. But he didn't need a whore for a father either. Junior was the only reason I didn't file the first time. I continued to look at Sam through the window.

I remembered the first few months during my pregnancy, he called every day and night. He tried to take a leave of absence just so he could be here for every doctor's appointment. He didn't want to miss a single moment of my pregnancy. He did manage to take a few weeks off as Junior was on his way. We both wanted to wait until the baby was born to find out if it was a boy or girl.

When I laid my eyes on Junior, I fell in love. I thanked God he looked like me; there were no features of Sam anywhere. After they placed Junior into my arms, I didn't want to let him go. Sam was too nervous to hold him. He was just glad that he had a son to carry on his last name. Once we brought Junior home, Sam was constantly holding him, changing his diapers, feeding him, and playing with him. He was a hands-on dad.

Then after several months, Sam went back to his old tricks. Sleeping with one female after another, trying his best to deny that he did anything with them. I knew better. When Sam was done playing with them and left, they would come to me secretly and drop off pictures of Sam being with them in a very sexual way.

I had gotten so fed with his affairs, I packed up Junior and left. I never told Billy why I had left him. If he knew then what he knows now, Sam would have been dead years ago. One of Sam's military friends had told me that my two uncles made a trip and kidnapped Sam for looking at another woman.

I always wanted to ask my uncles what happened when they went to track down Sam across the seas. I decided against it. Watching Sam play with his phone, I wondered what he was up to or planning this time? Who was he screaming at? Moments later, Sam got out and locked all the doors, carrying a few takeout bags. I would have to start my own private investigation as soon as he fell asleep. I heard Sam as he entered through the door.

"Rene, baby I'm back. Sorry it took me so long but traffic was kind of bad, so I had to wait. The food is still hot if you are still hungry. I'm starving. I also remembered that it has been so long since we had any time together. Tomorrow, how about we let Junior sleep over at one of his friend's houses, and we can rekindle some passion and romance." Sam looked eager for me to say yes.

"I will have to really think about it. After tonight, I don't know if I want that. After all these years with you and you still step outside of this marriage, and even before then, I am supposed to welcome you back into my life for you to take advantage of me? The first time I left your ass I should have stayed gone. I am still considering filing for a divorce."

Sam

I was taken completely by surprise at this news. There was no way in hell she was going to divorce me. We had been through way too much just to throw in the towel now. I would fight for my marriage until the day I died. Elizabeth would not destroy my family. I would see to it.

"Rene, baby let me talk to you. First, there will be no divorce. I can't lose my family. I committed these adulterous crimes, not you. I know that I messed up. It's my job to fix it and I will. Baby, you will see. I will fix our family and get things back on track. Things will be different; you will see. I don't want to waste the entire night fighting with you; let's just enjoy our dinner and take it one day at a time."

Rene

I had heard this story before. I was so fed up hearing it again. What I wanted to hear was that Sam would take his gun and blow Elizabeth's head off. Not some sad old fairytale ass story.

Chapter 10

Kingston

Billy and Kingston knew they'd better make a trip out to Colorado. They both had a funny feeling about Rene's situation. For them to help keep her safe, they needed to find out more about this mystery woman who had the hots for Sam.

Dr. Shelby hadn't stop calling Kingston since the day he met her years ago when Rene found out that she was pregnant with Junior. He was flattered that she was interested in him, and he didn't mind talking to her. Most times, however, he wished she would just back up. She would bug him about when he was going to take her out on a real date.

Even Tiana gave him hell about spending more time with Shelby. She said he needed to step out with a woman every now and again. Tiana approved of Dr. Shelby; they seemed to get along. Kingston knew if Tiana didn't approve, he would have to block Shelby's number.

The more he talked to Shelby, Kingston wondered if LillyMae would approve of the fact that he met a doctor. Just thinking about her always brought a smile to his face. Every time he saw Tiana's smile, it reminded him of LillyMae. He was grateful for the time they had got to spend before the good Lord called her home.

Kingston blamed his siblings for her death, not the cancer. Some people beat cancer. In his heart he knew she fought as long as she could. Kingston knew LillyMae would want him to go on with his life and still protect

Tiana. Once he heard Virginia leave, he got up to go check on her. Which meant he would have to tiptoe over to her house and leave a calling card for her. Jaxson was easy. He talked a good game but in reality, Jaxson was a chicken shit coward who was quick to call the police on people.

Walking into the living room, Kingston saw Tiana picking up Genesis' toys, trying to calm herself down.

"Hey honey, I heard the commotion that Virginia had caused. You don't have to protect or defend me. I am a grown man. I can take care of myself. You have that baby boy to raise and look after. I know you are working and going to college to get your degree. If you want me to leave, just say so and I will. I'm not going to get you and your son kicked out."

Tiana stopped and turned to face him, wishing that he would not say things like that. She already lost her grandmother. There was no way she was going to let him out of her sight.

"Now you just stop that devil talk; you are staying right here with us. You just got home. I know Grandma would want you here with us. To hell with what Virginia just said. That bitch is nosey. If I didn't know any better, I would think she is Jaxson's eyes and ears. I love having you here. Genesis does too. We all have a great time together."

Kingston opened his mouth to speak, but Tiana continued.

"It was my decision to keep him and be a single parent. I'm not the first and not the last. You are staying here. No more talk about you moving out. Okay?"

Kingston smiled behind her back. He referred to her as "little LillyMae", and what she said, went. There was no way he could argue with her. If even he tried to, she would win. After hearing her testimony, he decided to drop it. But he would take care of Virginia. She had upset his baby girl, and now she would pay for that mistake.

First, he needed to get dressed and make a few phone calls. Kingston was breaking the money he had saved up while in prison and had gotten paid to work a few other inmate cases. He invested his money in stocks and bonds when he got out.

Once he ran into Billy, they made even more money. While Tiana was out of the house, he would get on the internet to look for her a nice house and a better car. He planned to surprise her with it since her birthday was coming up. It would be close to her job and school.

Looking at Genesis, who was still sleeping, Kingston smiled. He loved that little boy. Tiana wanted to put him in childcare, but since Kingston had a lot of free time, he wanted Genesis to stay home with him. He looked so much like Tiana and LillyMae. They always had a great time together. Kingston saw his phone vibrating. Rolling his eyes at Dr. Shelby's calls, he decided to let it go to voicemail.

He had enough problems of his own. He would deal with her later. Right now, Tiana and Genesis needed him. As he looked at his phone, hoping she would give up this second time, she called him and texted him.

It took all of Kingston's nerves not to tell her to go find a sex toy. He was trying not to hurt her feelings, but she was pushing it big time. Kingston turned on the shower full blast to let the hot water massage his body. It had been a while since he had seen a doctor. Kingston always kept himself in great shape, working out on a regular basis. He stopped going to the gym because Genesis was his daily workout.

Finishing his shower and getting dressed to start the day, he knew Genesis would be waking up soon. Tiana might need his help to get him dressed and fed. It was a nice warm day out. He would take Genesis to the park while Tiana got the chance to rest for a few hours.

He really needed to call Billy to find out when they were going to take a trip out to Colorado to visit Rene. He would call Rene too. Maybe she could give him the name of this mystery lady who was causing trouble. Then he would have a lead on how to track her down.

Cleaning up his room and making sure it was nice and tidy so it was one less thing Tiana had to do, Kingston was ready to start the day.

Walking into the living room, Kingston noticed that Genesis was already giving his mama hell. Kingston tried his best not to giggle but that little boy was strong. He wasn't going to give Tiana a break. He could see how frustrated she was getting, so Kingston decided to give her a hand, but he just couldn't resist to add on.

"Brings back memories, doesn't it?" Kingston laughed.

"Uncle that is not funny. He can't go outside without getting dressed and he hasn't eaten anything yet. This boy is already working on my last good nerve. He acts like he is running things."

"Alright, I got it covered. Don't worry about it. I am happy to help you. You need a break and rest. I will take over from here." Kingston smiled.

Kingston's phone vibrated. He reached into his pocket to see who it was. Before he could respond to the caller, Genesis had already grabbed it and was making baby noises. Kingston laughed. Tiana just shook her head. Kingston took his phone from Genesis.

"Hello," Kingston answered.

"Hey Kingston, it's Billy. We need to meet up and talk but I can see your hands are full with Genesis, which reminds me that I need to stop by the store and buy him some gifts. The way he answers your phone, I think I will buy him one."

Kingston laughed. Genesis was only six months old. There was no way Tiana would let him have a phone at this young age. Knowing Billy, he would buy it.

"Billy, Genesis is only six months old. You can buy him a play phone that makes a lot of noise. That way he can stop bothering mine and his mama's phone. The boy loves to push buttons."

"Kingston, I know how old he is and I wasn't going to get him a real phone. Tiana isn't going to kick my old ass. How is she anyway?"

"She is fine; just working hard as usual. I was going to call Rene. Maybe she can give me information on who this woman is. I really need a lead to go on. Virginia also stopped by; Tiana gave her an ear full."

Billy

Billy wished that Kingston would just reveal himself to let his siblings know that he was out of prison. Instead of playing these silly ass mind games. He knew Kingston had his reasons for staying in the dark. LillyMae's children got what they deserved. He didn't know the whole story as to why there was so much bad blood between them, however.

Kingston never shared that part of his story with him. Billy figured that when he was ready to open that can of worms, he would. For now, all he could do was be supportive.

"Billy, I know Sam is still a punk ass bitch and his love affairs have not ended. I wish that Rene would just divorce his ass and move on with her life. She can do better, and if she's worried about raising Junior alone, she shouldn't be. We will be there for her." Kingston sounded like he wanted to take the drive himself.

"I know we will, but it's her decision. We will wait until she chooses on her own. You did bring up an excellent point. I would love to know who this bitch is too."

Kingston

That was not the response that Kingston wanted to hear. He also knew that Billy was right. They should wait and see what Rene would do. All Kingston wanted was to break a few of Sam's bones. The way he was feeling, he was looking for a new punching bag.

"Okay, we will wait and find out together, but I will tell you one thing: I won't wait forever. She is my family as much she is yours and I will not tolerate this bullshit. You keep me updated and let's meet tomorrow. Tiana will be at work and we will have the place to ourselves. Oh, wait a second. Genesis will be with me. I didn't want Tiana to put him in childcare."

"I understand. We can meet. I will have my driver come and take Tiana to work and school or wherever she needs to go. It will give him something to do instead of waiting outside in the parking lot."

"Alright. See you then. And another thing: don't go play detective behind my back."

Billy just disconnected the call.

Chapter 11

Rene

I couldn't sleep at all after thinking about what Sam had said to me last night about there being no divorce. Was that an idle threat that he was making toward me? I never heard him say things like that before.

Sitting at the table in silence, I didn't hear Junior come into the kitchen. He could see I was worried about something and it frightened him. I was never quiet on a Saturday morning and he wasn't used to getting up this early either.

"Hey Ma, are you okay? It's not like you to be silent and distant. You always cook a big breakfast."

"I'm fine sweetheart; it just that I got so much on my mind lately and if you want to, I still can cook you a nice hearty breakfast." I smiled at my son.

"It's okay. It's not fun when you don't have the music blasting and you singing and doing your funny dances. I know when something is bothering you or when you are mad or upset."

"Junior I will never lie to you. I am fine. With school and work, I gotta remember that I am no longer in my twenties. I can't keep up with this generation like I used to." I laughed.

"If you say so. I can eat one of these breakfast bowls and call it a morning," Junior said.

"I can do better than that. I can treat you both out to a hearty breakfast and some family fun time. No need to sit around the house and waste this beautiful day," Sam suggested as he entered the kitchen.

Junior and I looked at each other. I gave a slight smile to reassure my son that it was alright. I was willing to go out and have some fun.

Junior

Junior smiled back at his mother, not sure what exactly was going on with his parents. He knew Rene better than anyone.

He would call his great Uncles Kingston and Billy on three-way. Junior didn't like when Rene was feeling sad. He knew from her facial expression that she was on the verge of tears. Leaving his parents alone to talk, he quietly walked out of the kitchen.

Rene

"Good morning beautiful; I know we didn't get to finish our conversation last night and that's my fault. We both are a little stressed out about what I have done. But I meant what I said: we are not getting a divorce. We have a son to raise. We made a promise to God, and we will honor that," Sam preached.

I didn't know if I wanted to smack him or laugh at him. The more he talked, the more pissed off I was getting. I wanted to scream and throw every single knife at him. I didn't want Junior to hear the book of words I had for him. It would have to wait until later. I couldn't ruin this day for my son.

"Good morning to you as well," I answered. "I'm really not in the mood to go out, but since its Saturday, I will. I will not ruin this day for Junior. He can't see me this upset, but I am not done cursing you out. While we are gone and will be in public eye, I will act civil, but if I see that bitch Elizabeth, I cannot guarantee my fucking actions."

"Rene, all I want is to spend time with my family and make you happy again. I don't want to spend this day or any other day fighting with you. I love you too much for that. I will prove it to you."

I just rolled my eyes. As I was trying to walk past him, Sam blocked my way, grabbed me, and pulled me in a for a romantic kiss. He was really trying to prove that he was determined to make this marriage work.

Elizabeth

Sitting across the street in an unmarked car, Elizabeth watched the couple with her binoculars, outraged that Sam would betray her this way. She wasn't going to let Sam go that easy. It was time for a showdown.

"I'm the one that needs a kiss like that every morning, and to have him holding me. Not her. Why is he being an asshole toward me? He didn't treat me this bad until she turned on me. I was willing to share him with her, but she had to fuck that up. I let go of Leah's daddy. I'd be damned if I let go of her soon to be stepdaddy," Elizabeth seethed.

Elizabeth really wanted to get out of the car, bust through their house, and rip Rene's head off. Rene was living the life that she was meant to have.

She really had to stop Sam from making the biggest mistake of his life. Elizabeth fantasized about knocking Rene out, taking her body and tying her up to a railroad track, and watching her get run over by a train.

Didn't Rene know that Sam had feelings for Elizabeth? Sam was only pretending to love Rene for Junior's sake. Elizabeth was Sam's true love. Elizabeth couldn't wait to marry him. She continued to sit across the street, watching them like a hawk. What Sam needed was a snow bunny, and not some project drug street trash.

Elizabeth wasn't afraid of Rene. She knew she talked a tough game, but she would love to show her just how much of a badass she really was.

Junior

Pacing back and forth in his room with his phone in his hands, Junior debated if he should make the call. He hated when people hid things from him. Both his parents taught him to stay out of grown folks' business. He could respect that there were certain things that children should not get involved in. But if he didn't make the call and try to get some answers, it would keep nagging at him.

Dialing his uncle Billy's number first, then three-waying Kingston, Junior decided it wouldn't hurt to have a man-to-man talk.

"Hello," Billy answered.

"Hello," Kingston answered.

"Hi, it's me Junior. I was calling because I really need to talk about my mom. She doesn't seem happy at all. A few nights ago, I heard her and Dad arguing and I got the feeling that Elizabeth is the reason why she has been so upset."

Capturing their attention, they both listened very carefully to what Junior had to say.

"This Elizabeth is the woman that is a friend of your parents?" Kingston asked.

"Yeah, but since we moved, dad has been spending a lot of time with her and Leah. That's her daughter. At first, I thought she was cool and nice until she really wanted to hang out with my dad more than mom. Maybe mom is just feeling left out or something. She hasn't been acting like herself and I am worried about her. Can't the two of you help her? Bring Tiana and Genesis out to visit us. Maybe she's just homesick."

"Junior, do you know how to get this Elizabeth's phone number? I would like to talk to her," Billy asked.

"Sure, I can get it from my parent's phone and text you back with her contact information. Uncle Kingston, do you think that Tiana can call my mom and talk to her? Maybe that will cheer her up," Junior suggested.

"Yeah I can get her to call. It's been a while since they talked. I will tell her now to call her. And when you get that information, give it to me as well. I will need to speak with Elizabeth also. And Junior? Don't worry; everything is fine," Billy babbled.

"Junior, thanks for calling us. We will make a trip out there soon. I'll see if Tiana wants to tag along. I will check her schedule and get back to you," Kingston agreed.

"Thanks; I feel a lot better knowing that you are all coming to visit and spend time with us. She will be glad to see everyone. I better get going. We are supposed to go out for breakfast and have family fun time."

Chapter 12

Rene

I pulled away from Sam. I wasn't ready to cave into his temptation yet. Or fall for any more of his lies. I was already confused about my mixed feelings for him. I really needed to start growing a backbone, and there was only one person who could help me do that: Tiana.

Tiana was my favorite cousin. She always spoke her mind freely. There weren't too many people who could handle her mouth or her attitude. The last time Tiana spoke her mind was when she called me and told me she was having a baby and scared out of her mind. Last time Tiana came out to visit, she stayed for a few months to help take care of me. She cursed Sam out every chance she got.

How could I get through the day knowing that I was hurting inside? Going into my closet to pick out a nice outfit that I would be comfortable in, I decided on my black and white sweatsuit.

I went to the bathroom to take a quick shower and get dressed. After applying my makeup, I felt satisfied with my natural look. Smiling to myself for the first time, I decided I would give Tiana a call when she returned home. Walking out the bathroom, I saw Sam standing there with the biggest grin on his face. He hadn't grinned like that since the first time I met him. What was the grin for?

I tried to avoid him, but every time I tried to move past him, he would block me. I wasn't in the mood to play wrestle with him or even hear what he had to say. All I wanted was to enjoy my Saturday without having these mixed emotions. Another part of me wanted to forgive Sam so bad for what he did to me.

Every instinct in my body told me something was not right. Sam was keeping a secret from me. And Elizabeth was still lurking somewhere trying to seek revenge on me. I just couldn't shake the uneasy feeling.

"Baby you look radiant today," Sam commented.

"Thank you; it's been a while since I have had the chance to put together a different look. I thought today I could rock something sporty."

"I love any look on you." Sam smiled. "How about when Junior goes to bed or spends the night at one of his friends' house, I can show you a magical night? I know I made a lot of promises to you and didn't always make good on them, but this time I want to keep every promise," Sam stated.

"Look Sam; I know you want to try and make this marriage work. I just feel there is more to this story than you are willing to admit." I continued to stare at him.

"Rene, how many times do we have to go over this? I have told you everything. I wouldn't lie to you about anything. All I want is to start over from a clean slate. Make you happy and earn your trust again. It's a nice day out. We all look good today. I don't want to waste it by talking about my past mistakes. Let's just move forward with our lives."

Sam

Leaning close to give Rene a kiss on the cheek, I really did want to make our marriage work and move forward. There was no way that I was going to let Elizabeth break up this happy home. I was keeping a secret from Rene, but what she didn't know wouldn't hurt her.

I would just have to find a way to keep Elizabeth's mouth shut. I was determined to get rid of her. I was looking into Rene's eyes hoping like hell she would drop it and say, "let's move on with our lives". Just as I was about to lean in to steal another kiss, we heard Junior yelling, "GET AWAY FROM OUR HOUSE, ELIZABETH!" Rene and I ran out of the room and downstairs to where Junior was standing outside looking at Elizabeth smiling at us.

Rene punched Elizabeth in her mouth, causing it to bleed. Junior and I struggled to pull Rene away from Elizabeth. All the neighbors come outside to watch the fight. Rene called Elizabeth every curse word that she could think of.

"Come on baby, she isn't worth you going to jail," I said.

"Mom, come on! I don't want to see you in handcuffs. Let her go; Mom, please let her go," Junior cried out.

Rene didn't hear a word either of us said. She was trying to tear Elizabeth apart for showing up at our home.

We kept struggling with Rene until we heard police sirens coming down the street. Elizabeth finally wrenched away and left.

"Baby, calm down. Go inside with Junior. Let me handle the police okay? Go wash that beautiful face of yours. Junior, go help your mama while I handle this situation."

Junior led his mother inside the house to make sure she wasn't hurt, then he walked back to the door where I was talking to the officers.

Junior

Junior was thanking God that his mom was safe. He knew Elizabeth was the reason why her behavior had changed these last few months. After taking that beatdown, maybe Elizabeth would stay away and leave his family alone. If not, then he would get her contact information and give it to his great uncles, Billy and Kingston.

There was one remaining question that still bothered him: what had caused his mom to attack Elizabeth? She never disrespected anyone as far as Junior saw. Junior continued to watch as his father talked to the police.

Chapter 13

Elizabeth

"That bitch might have gotten the best of me, but she hasn't seen or heard the last of me!" Elizabeth screamed.

Highly upset that Sam wouldn't come to her rescue, nor once even bothered to call and check to see how she was feeling infuriated her. Everything was fine until that brat of his just had to come outside and spot her. He made a big deal out of nothing. Elizabeth didn't do anything wrong. All she wanted was to see her man, Sam.

It was time to turn up the heat. She couldn't let Rene win or outshine her. She lost that battle already with Leah's daddy. However, Elizabeth wanted Sam and only Sam. She was originally going to invite Junior to come and be a part of her family when Sam divorced Rene. After this little stunt, he could join his mother in the afterlife.

Sam

After I was done talking to the police, I went inside to talk to Rene. She couldn't possibly blame me for any of this. I didn't tell Elizabeth to come over to our home. I had no idea why she was outside. She would not ruin this day or our time together. We would continue with our family plans.

"Hey baby, are you alright?" I asked.

Rene didn't speak for several minutes.

"No, I'm not fine. I can't believe that bitch came to our house and disrespected me like that. This is all your damn fault. Something had to have happened between the two of you, and you're not telling me what it is. I've had friends for years and when the friendship was over, it was over. They didn't act the way that crazy white bitch is acting!" Rene screamed. "Did you sleep with her? I need for you to tell me the truth now and I won't bother trying to find out later. Sam, now is the time to come clean with me."

I knew I had to keep my cool and lie about the affair with Elizabeth. If I didn't, Rene would divorce me and take Junior with her and that would be the end of my life.

"Baby for the last time, I didn't do anything with this woman. All I was trying to be was a friend and help her out. Nothing more or less. I promise you, there is nothing going on between Elizabeth and me."

Rene just looked at me like she knew I was lying. I was praying that she wouldn't go behind my back and start snooping. Trying to keep this secret was a lot harder than I thought it would be.

There were two powerful men that could get rid of my problem. That was the only way to protect my family. Just the thought of making this conference call was dreadful, but I figured I might as well man up and call Billy and Kingston.

I knew that they hated my guts, but they loved Rene and Junior and would do anything to protect them. If I wanted to earn back my family's love, trust and respect, it was time to get rid of Elizabeth. I didn't want her to die; just to get out of our lives.

"Rene, you are going to give yourself a stroke or a heart attack now; I need you to calm down. She is gone. On Monday, we will get a protective order against her.

We will block her from our phones, social media accounts and everything. We will go to Junior's school and let them know who she is and what she looks like just in case she tries to mess with him or something. I will protect this family."

Rene

I knew Sam was full of bullshit. There was no way I was going to trust his word. It was time to find out the connection between Sam and Elizabeth. With Tiana's help, I would get to the bottom of this. If there was more to his lies, I would have no choice but to divorce Sam and take Junior with me. This time there would be no coming back.

"Sam, I just can't help but feel there is more to this story. I have been more than willing to give you a chance after chance to tell me the fucking truth. I would rather be hurt with the truth than destroyed with a sweet lie."

I ran out of the kitchen crying my eyes out. I went into the guest bathroom and locked the door behind me, crying and screaming "I HATE YOU!" as Sam pounded on the door begging for me to open it to let him in.

Sam

Walking away to give her some time to calm down and cool off, I grabbed my keys, telling Junior to look out for his mother until I returned.

What Elizabeth pulled was the last straw. I had already made it very clear that it was over. Already feeling my blood pressure on the rise because of my affair with Elizabeth, I really wanted to beat the living hell out of her. I knew not to put my hands on a woman; I raised Junior not to hit a woman no matter how angry he got.

Junior

Pulling out of the driveway and speeding down the street, leaving a cloud of smoke behind him, Junior could hear his father's tires screech. Junior didn't know whether to call his uncles back and tell them what happened or not. Moments later, Rene came out of the bathroom in search for Sam. Junior looked at her with concern.

Sam

I took out my cell phone to unblock Elizabeth's number. I was going to give her a piece of my mind and show her I meant business.

Dialing her number, she answered after a few rings.

"Hello darling."

"Look, I am coming over. We need to talk and clear up something. What I am about to tell you, I really mean."

Elizabeth

Sam hung up in her face, but Elizabeth couldn't have been happier. He was going to tell her that he had come to his senses and was filing for a divorce. They were going to get married and be a family: just him, her, and Leah.

Elizabeth rushed to the bathroom to wash her face and make herself presentable before he arrived. She couldn't wait to see Sam again and make love to him. She craved him so much. She was going to make him the luckiest man in the world.

Moments later, Sam arrived. Elizabeth greeted him at the door.

"Sam, I am so happy to see you! It's been so long. How about we go upstairs and make love? Forget all this crazy nonsense." Elizabeth smiled, hoping like hell he would say yes.

"Have you lost your damn mind?" Sam yelled.

Chapter 14

Kingston

Just spending a few hours at the park with Genesis, Kingston knew it was close to lunch time and he was getting hungry. Genesis was having a wonderful time playing in the sandbox with the other babies.

Kingston always wanted kids of his own, but helping raise Tiana and Genesis was good enough. He thought that he would have a family with Rebecca, but it didn't work out. Before he was released from prison, however, he found out that he had two sons. Rebecca refused to allow him to be a part of their lives. From what he was told, LillyMae got to see them once when they were infants.

She and Rebecca exchanged words, and things got pretty heated. Rebecca vanished without a trace, taking the boys with her. Kingston had no idea what their names were. The only way to find them was to find her.

Tiana had already made up her mind that when she saw Rebecca, she would punch her in the face. Kingston just shrugged it off; he knew she was speaking from anger. Picking up Genesis, Kingston got ready to take him back to Tiana for lunch. For now, just being an uncle was good enough for him.

He would pay Virginia a visit; not in person - he would leave a calling card for her. He wanted to face off with Jaxson. There was no way he going to escape from him this time. Jaxson talked a tough game while

Kingston was in prison. Kingston wanted to see that bad boy talk in person. Kingston loved his family dearly. He just couldn't understand why they never returned any of it. Tiana reassured him that they were a bunch of evil jackasses.

No need to love or be bothered with people who don't want to be bothered with you. That caused him to think about Shelby. He knew she didn't deserve to be treated that way. Once she found out he had been in prison for thirty years, would she still want to be around him or leave him? Kingston's mind lingered on Shelby for a minute, then he focused back on LillyMae.

It had been a while since he visited LillyMae's grave. Kingston thought about going to go visit her and having a chat with her. He needed her guidance. He felt so lost without her. Thank God for Tiana and Genesis, who welcomed him with open arms. Without them, he wouldn't know how to carry on with his life. Since LillyMae passed, Kingston's heart broke every time he thought about his beloved mother.

Kingston held Genesis as he walked back to Tiana. She was blasting music in the kitchen while cooking. Tiana always overcooked a lot of food. That was one of the things that she had inherited from her grandmother. Feeling his phone vibrate in his pocket, Kingston turned down the music so he could hear.

"Hello uncle Kingston. It's me, Rene. I can't reach Uncle Billy, so I called you. I almost went to jail. That bitch Elizabeth came to my house and I just went the fuck off. I got the strangest feeling that Sam slept with this bitch, but he refuses to tell me the truth. Are you still coming? Maybe Tiana and Genesis can come out here too. It would be nice to see my cousin again."

Things in Colorado had gotten out of control. Maybe Rene was right. Maybe Sam had slept with this woman and was lying about it. Kingston knew if he ever found out that he lied and broke another promise, he was going to kick his teeth down his throat. For now, he needed to calm down Rene before she really went to jail.

"Rene, calm down. We are coming out there to spend time with you. Unless you got some solid evidence that Sam has done anything with this woman, there really is no proof. You are a smart young lady; always trust your gut. If you feel different, act on it. But think before you do."

"You're right. I don't know where Sam went anyway. He's not answering his phone. Elizabeth just messed up my entire day. I look so cute and adorable too."

Kingston knew that Tiana and Rene were indeed related; Tiana always said the same thing. He shook his head. As he continued to listen to Rene rant and rave about her marriage with Sam, Kingston didn't understand why she wouldn't file for a divorce and leave his sorry ass alone. She was a beautiful woman. Any man would be happy to be with her.

Kingston thought for a second. It wasn't like Billy not to answer Rene's calls. Kingston would call him after lunch. The food Tiana was cooking was making his mouth water and stomach growl. In his mind, an uncle's job was never done. He was honored that Rene came to him and talked whenever she needed that family love and support.

After a few more minutes of talking to each other, he was praying that he had calmed Rene down. He would send a text message to Sam. He wasn't happy to hear that Rene almost caught a case behind his sorry ass. He would also make a few phone calls to some of his old partners in crime. He planned to send them out to Colorado to spy on Sam and find this Elizabeth bitch.

Looking out the window, he saw Jaxson's truck pull up. Kingston walked into the kitchen to give Tiana the heads up before he disappeared down the hall into his room. He wasn't ready to be seen yet.

Tiana

Giving Genesis his favorite toy as she put him down into his play pen, Tiana walked into the living room wondering why Jaxson was here.

"Tiana hey niece; what's going on? Virginia told me what had happened between the two of you. I want to know why Kingston is hiding from us?" Jaxson asked.

Tiana had to take a deep breath before she cursed his ass out.

"I don't have to tell you shit. As far as whatever Virginia told your ass, I don't care. Neither of you has treated him like family. He's not fucking with you or her sorry ass. Just leave him alone."

"Little girl, I'm your uncle. You don't disrespect me like that or talk to me like you don't have any home training. You can talk to those niggas on the streets like that, but not me."

Tiana turned to open the door. She didn't want to continue to talk to him. She was at the point where she was about to throw a punch or two. Before she could move past Jaxson, he grabbed her and spun her around, grinding his teeth.

"Let go of me, before I bust your ass! Fuck you, nigga," Tiana screamed.

Jaxson raised his hand and smacked Tiana in the face. That was when Kingston came rushing toward him and exchanged blows. Tiana grabbed Genesis and ran into his room, giving him his bottle. She ran back into the living room, yelling at both of them to stop before someone called the cops.

Kingston picked Jaxson up and body slammed him to the floor. Tiana was frozen stiff. She couldn't move even if she wanted to. It was like watching WWE wrestling, with Kane and The Undertaker tearing each other apart. Jaxson was no match for Kingston, however. Kingston was too quick. Tiana could see that Jaxson's left eye was starting to swell up.

"Uncle Kingston, stop. Just let him go."

Kingston

Kingston looked at Tiana before he took one more swing at Jaxson. He thought about how LillyMae would react, knowing that her two sons were fighting like dogs in heat.

"Now you see me, and yeah, I am free, but if you ever touch my damn baby again, your ass is dead. 'Cause I will kill you and make sure when I send you to your grave to say hello to Mama and Chase for me," Kingston warned.

Jaxson stared at Kingston like couldn't believe it. He slowly got up and staggered across the room, not saying another word. Kingston watched as Jaxson climbed into his truck.

The last time Tiana had seen Kingston open a can of whip ass was when Willie, her father, had spanked her and left a bruise. She had always known that Kingston had a dark gangster side; she just didn't know how dark until now. Kingston continued to look out the window.

Kingston knew that Jaxson was going to start planning something shady and sneaky. If he didn't know any better, he would go to Virginia and let her know that Kingston was out and where he had been living. Next time he put his hands on Tiana, however, Kingston would make good on his promise. May God have mercy on his soul.

Chapter 15

Elizabeth

Elizabeth wasn't expecting this reaction from Sam. He was supposed to be comforting her and holding her. She wanted to hear that he was leaving Rene to be with her and Leah. This was not the ways things were supposed to be. She would fight Rene tooth and nail to get Sam.

"Sam, why are you treating me this way after all I did for you? I sucked your dick, cooked all your favorite meals, listened to your problems with Rene, and on top of that I am the best lover you had in your entire life!" Elizabeth cried out.

Sam

I just looked at her, thinking to myself how pathetic she was making herself seem. How was she playing victim? She was the one who had started all of this in the first place. If anyone was a victim in this case, it was me. She kept trying to convince me to leave Rene, but it was a waste of time.

"Elizabeth, don't act so surprised. I am a married man with a family to support. I told you I will never leave my wife for you. Look, it was only sex. I didn't tell you to catch feelings for me. That's your fault you did that. It was supposed to be a fun thing; now the fun is over for us. I am staying with my wife. You can deal with it or not. You better stay away from my family. I'm not attracted to white women. You are not even my type; never have been. Move on with your life and take Leah out of Colorado or move on to the next sucker. I'm not ever going to be with you again. Understand the words that are coming out of my mouth because this is the last time I am going to say this to you. Don't make me take action against you."

Elizabeth

Elizabeth was in complete shock. How dare he use her like a cheap whore that he picked up off the corner? He couldn't treat her this way. She would not allow it. Not this time. For once, she would go after what she wanted. Nobody could stop her; not even Sam. As Sam turned to leave, Elizabeth jumped up and started kissing him. Sam struggled to get her off of him. Elizabeth felt like she was losing her mind. Finally, he got her off.

"Elizabeth, get the hell off of me. Have you lost your fucking mind you, crazy ass bitch!" Sam yelled.

Elizabeth laughed at him. She knew he wanted her as much as she wanted him. Sam was just playing hard to get. She would play along for now.

"You know Sam, falling in love with a married man can make you do some crazy things. You can say whatever you want, or deny your feelings for me, but we both know the truth." She continued to laugh.

Sam

I had no idea what she was implying nor did I wanted to stick around to find out. All I knew was that, come Monday morning, I was going to the courthouse to get a protective order against her. Watching Elizabeth laugh, I now knew what a real fatal attraction could lead to. The way Elizabeth was behaving and acting like a mad woman, I knew getting rid of her would take more than a protective order.

Rene

I felt better after talking to Kingston. I wasn't going to waste this Saturday sitting in the house being upset. Junior and I could still spend time together. Sam would have to catch up with us later. I owed it to myself to go out and have some family fun time. I'd be damned if Elizabeth thought she could take my place. Going into the bathroom to wash my face and reapply my makeup, I could feel my blood pressure cooling down.

Feeling refreshed coming out of the bathroom, I called out Junior's name. We sat down to discuss what he would like to do. It was about time that we started to act like a family again.

Sam

I walked in looking at Rene and Junior laughing. That was what I loved to come home to. No stress or drama. I would do anything to protect them. This was the life I always dreamed of. Then I started to feel bad. How could I betray my family this way? I was selfish, taking advantage of Rene. She was a loving wife and mother. She didn't deserve that.

I felt like crying. How could I be this stupid? This was not how a man was supposed to behave. I had never felt more shamed than I did at that moment. I walked over to join my family to see what the laughs and smiles were about. I vowed internally to be the man that Rene deserved. I took a seat next to my wife, taking her hands into mine and kissing them. I looked at Junior, smiling.

"Hey, you two are having a grand old time. I'm ready to get out of this house and have some fun times. We can go bowling, movies, maybe grab some lunch and dinner at an all-you-can-eat restaurant."

Rene and Junior agreed that it was time to get out and start acting like a family. However, Rene thought it best that I pack up and move into the guest room until I could really prove to her that she could trust me. I turned to her.

"Baby I need to tell you something before we leave. I want you to know that I really do love you. We can make this work."

Rene

I didn't like the sound of this. Sending Junior to the car before we left, I turned to Sam. There was no way he was getting off this easy.

"Alright Sam; out with it. I want to know what is going on and don't say nothing because I know there is something going on between you and Elizabeth."

"Honey, there is nothing going on between us. I wanted to tell you that I went to go see her today to let her know on Monday that I will file a protective order against her. I saw how terribly upset you were moments ago. I've got to protect this family. I'll be damned if I let her or anyone hurt you. If you want, I think you should file one as well."

I wasn't going to file a protective order against her ass until I got to the bottom of the truth. Sam had his way of dealing with things and I had mine.

"Sam, that will not stop her from coming after us or mainly coming after you. If you think it's best, then fine I will go with you to file for one but I will not file one against her."

Sam

I didn't understand why she didn't want to file with me; we had Junior to protect. I knew Rene well enough to know when she was plotting revenge. I just didn't know when she would make her move. I could feel Rene's dangerous side coming out. When her dark side appeared, it wasn't safe to be around her.

"Sam when we get back home, I really would appreciate it if you moved into the guest bedroom. I really need to be alone and think things through. I strongly feel that you are not telling me everything and I don't believe that our marriage will make it. Only God has the final say whether we should stay together or not. For now, I don't want to talk about it. Junior is waiting for us to put on our happy faces and pretend to be happy. I will do it for his sake," Rene stated.

I felt my heart breaking. No matter what I did or said, Rene refused to change her mind about this divorce. I couldn't lose my family. There were two people who could get Rene to change her mind in order to save my marriage. I would have to confess my sins to God and Billy. They were the only two Rene would listen to.

Rene

I knew that I had hurt his feelings. I didn't know what else to do or say to him at this point. In my mind, all Sam did was lie and cheat on me. I didn't trust him. All the love, respect, and compassion I once had for him was gone.

Chapter 16

Jaxson

Jaxson drove over to Virginia's house to show her the beating that Kingston just put on him. He thought about calling the police and pressing charges, but he knew that Tiana would defend him, telling the police that Kingston defended her because Jaxson put his hands on her.

Jaxson's entire body hurt. He could feel the swelling beginning from his eyes, as well as a gigantic headache. He could see Virginia in the kitchen pretending to cook. The only thing she could cook that didn't make people sick that was her famous chilly mac. He knew once she saw his face that she was going to go crazy. He winced in pain as he slowly climbed out of his truck.

Virginia

Virginia saw Jaxson and was wondering what in the world had happened. He barely made it up the steps. Having all kinds of thoughts running through her mind, she wondered if she should get him some medical attention and call her husband Raymond.

"Jaxson, good Lord! What happened to you?" Virginia said with a concern that he might have been robbed.

"Kingston is what happened to me. I went over to Tiana's house and we exchanged words. When she turned to walk away from me, I grabbed her. That's when he appeared out of nowhere and we fought," Jaxson explained.

Virginia knew that Tiana was lying about Kingston's whereabouts. She also knew how overprotective she could be when it came to him.

"Come on into the house. I will call Chyna. She needs to come and look at your face. I know you won't go to the hospital to have them to look at you," Virginia stated.

Helping Jaxson into the house, Virginia couldn't believe that Kingston was out of prison. Now she was wondering if he would come after her. Raymond didn't know how to fight. She would talk to him about getting a gun. Just because he was an ordained minister and chef didn't mean he couldn't protect his family.

Kingston

Kingston finally calmed his nerves. He heard Genesis crying, which let him know he wasn't done with his duties as an uncle. He went to check on him and saw that Tiana just finished changing his diaper. He walked up behind her, patted her on the head and kissed her cheek. Taking Genesis from her hands, they all exchanged pleasant smiles. Kingston knew that he had to apologize for his violent behavior and explain why he let that devil Jaxson make him come out of his comfort zone.

Listening to Genesis laugh as Kingston tickled him, he placed him on the floor with his favorite blanket and all his toys spread all over the place. Kingston couldn't believe how fast he was growing. He reminded him so much of Tiana when she was a baby.

He turned to Tiana. "Listen honey I just want to say I am sorry for what had happened. That damn Jaxson got away with pushing my buttons. When I heard you scream, I just lost my cool. Usually, I don't do that. It reminded me of back when your grandma would be with these no-good ass niggas. They would beat on her. I was the family protector. I would come home and beat their asses for hitting her. She would try and pretend it was nothing, but I knew better. I'd be damned if they hurt her again," Kingston confessed.

Tiana

Tiana understood what it felt like to get abused by men. Genesis' father Thurman would try to fight her even when she was pregnant. He would get drunk then come and start trouble. The further she got in her pregnancy, the worse it became.

Tiana decided one day it was time to leave. She couldn't take it anymore. When he left for work, she sold everything in the house. LillyMae and Uncle Chase must have been watching over her because she got approved for her first apartment through government housing.

That was the best day of her life, packing her clothes quickly before Thurman came home for lunch. That was the day she learned how to be an independent woman standing on her own feet, unlike her older sister Sarah Jean who couldn't live without a man to save her life.

Tiana knew how to survive many tragedies: the death of her beloved grandmother, living with friends, and even her mother Chyna, who had pushed her into a glass shelf. Thank God she didn't look up when it happened; otherwise, she would have gone blind. When Tiana ran away from home to be with her new boyfriend and live with his brother, that only lasted for two weeks when she found out he was cheating on her.

Having no real friends that she could trust, Tiana looked at the world as black and white. Nobody protected or wanted to be around her. She always thought something was wrong with her.

Walking to school one day, she knew she being followed. Being cautious about her whereabouts, she zigged and zagged. Thankfully, she made it to school without getting kidnapped.

Still wondering who the mystery man was who was following her, she sat in class trying to put the thought out of her mind. She got called out of class. There he was again: the mystery man who had been following her. Why would he be here at her school? For a slight moment, she was about to get excited. She thought it was her uncle Kingston.

When she heard the mystery man speak, it wasn't Kingston at all. But he looked so much like him. Tiana was nervous, walking briskly to greet the man. He introduced himself as her uncle Billy. Kingston had reached out to him because he thought that she needed his protection until he was released from prison.

Letting out a deep breath, the mention of Kingston's name made her feel better. They had lost contact after LillyMae died and Chyna kept moving, strung out on drugs until someone reported her to child protective services. That's when she decided to get her life back on track and left her no good boyfriend alone.

Tiana and Billy decided to meet every morning before school, during lunch breaks, and after school. They talked a lot. He even bought her a cell phone. Tiana kept it on silent and only texted when she could. She would call him when Chyna left her alone. Tiana finally made a friend that she could turn to in her time of need. Billy never told her how he and Kingston were related. From her understanding they were half-brothers.

There were so many things about Kingston's life that were misunderstood about him. Tiana was grateful to have him in her life but she would be glad when he found a woman to settle down with and be happy. Kingston had swag and a voice that most women fell madly in love with.

"Uncle Kingston, no need to apologize. Jaxson had it coming. Nobody is to blame but him. I can tell Rene this story when I call her later on today. Speaking of stories, when are you going to go out on a date? Stop hiding from women; nothing is wrong with dinner, movie, and dating." Tiana laughed as she finished cooking lunch.

Kingston

Kingston couldn't help but to join in on the laughter. Walking back into the living room he saw Genesis had played himself to sleep. Thinking about Shelby, he wondered if he should get back to the dating scene again. He hadn't been in a serious relationship since Rebecca.

He had questions that only she could answer. She left and took their sons with her years before LillyMae's untimely death. Kingston remembered when Rebecca came back with the baby. LillyMae told him she named the baby Desmond. What was his other son's name? Rebecca was known to be with a man then leave, only to come back pregnant and leave again.

Kingston remembered that she wanted to have a baby so bad with him. When he finally gave her what she wanted, she left him heartbroken. While Genesis was sleeping, he decided he would need to make a trip to Virginia's house to let her know that she was next on his list.

Chapter 17

Elizabeth

Elizabeth still couldn't believe that Sam used her for sex, comfort, and friendship. All of that for nothing, just to please Rene, who didn't deserve him. She wondered if she should give Rene a fair warning that she was coming after Sam, whether she liked it or not.

Elizabeth wondered if Rene knew that Sam had been sleeping with her for months.

Telling her would be way too easy. She would need proof that she was telling the truth. Even though Elizabeth couldn't have any more children, she would have to cash in on a few favors. When she broke up Sam's happy marriage and married him, she would wait a few weeks and tell him she had a miscarriage.

If Sam wouldn't leave Rene, then Elizabeth would make Rene leave Sam. Sam would be Elizabeth's husband. Taking out her phone, Elizabeth knew the right person who could help her pull off this perfect plan. She owed Elizabeth a big-time favor.

Elizabeth dialed the number. She'd burned a lot of bridges and lost a lot of friends. They turned their backs on her when she turned state evidence over to the prosecutor and took a plea deal. Elizabeth testified against them. While serving time in prison, she received a lot of threatening letters. The other inmates double-teamed her. Elizabeth really couldn't fight back due to her seizures.

Serving a five-year prison term was pure hell for Elizabeth. No one would come visit her or return her letters. They always came back Return to Sender. Her friend didn't answer the call.

Elizabeth contemplated another plan, which was to trick Sam into coming back; maybe blackmail him into having sex. She'd always heard that black men were the best sex partners. Elizabeth didn't believe it until she started sleeping with Sam. He fucked the shit out of her, making her scream his name over and over.

She could still taste his dick inside of her mouth; the way he moved, grabbed her head, pushing his dick inside her mouth. Elizabeth's jaws were sore, but as long as she could taste his sweet chocolate, that was all that mattered. The first time she sucked his dick she thought she would choke on it. That's what she needed now: Sam's dick.

Elizabeth touched herself, pretending it was Sam's hand that was rubbing her body. Closing her eyes, she started thinking back to the way Sam used to whisper in her ears as he was fucking her from behind. He always made her feel special, like she was somebody important. She quickly snapped out of her trance when she heard Leah screaming her name.

Elizabeth loved her daughter, but she needed a father in her life. The perfect father for her would be Sam. It was up to Elizabeth to bring him home.

Rene

"Rene, baby I clearly understand how you feel but I don't want to move into the guest room. I need to be in the same room with you. I can't sleep without you. I don't mean to sound pushy; you mean the world to me. I want to make our marriage work. I am proving that to you by getting a protective order against Elizabeth. I'm showing you that I mean business. I will not take you for granted ever again," Sam stated.

"Sam, I see that you want to take matters into your hands. However, I feel that you are keeping something from me when it comes to Elizabeth's crazy ass. Tell me the truth now and I can deal with it. I don't want no surprises later. I have been trying my best to shake this horrible feeling that I have, and you just keep ignoring the main question that I have a right to know."

"Baby I swear to you there is nothing going on between us. Elizabeth is in love with me. I'm not attracted to white women; never have been. I might have been curious how their sex game is, but I would never in my life would want to be with one. I don't know what kind of feelings you have that is eating at you. I love you Rene, and only you. I will prove that to you. I know that I am to blame for this; I'm trying to be the husband that you deserve," Sam pleaded.

"Sam, I have what they called wife's intuition so I know when something is not right. Either you are going to tell me the truth behind this crazy ass white girl, or I will go to my resources and get the truth."

Sam

I knew that Rene was not playing. She would do whatever it took to get the information that she needed in order to get to plan B. Trying to get Rene to trust my word was going to be harder than I thought. Not saying anything more, I just let her have her space.

I hated that I had that affair with Elizabeth; now I couldn't get rid of her. I did agree with Rene. A protective order would not stop her from coming after me. What more could I do besides let the law handle this stalker?

Shelby

Shelby really wanted a relationship with Kingston. She had been texting and calling his phone all day but he refused to answer her calls or messages. Maybe she was being too pushy. She could call either Rene or Tiana. Maybe they could help her figure out why Kingston was being so cold toward her.

What more did he want her to do beside call or text him? When she did, she seemed to do most of the talking. She wanted to know more about him. She talked about herself enough; there really wasn't more to tell him. She wanted to hear his voice. She didn't want to turn into a crazy girlfriend and investigate him. She didn't want to scare him off.

How could she get him to open up to her? All she wanted was to get to know him and become his friend; God willing, someday become his wife. Shelby didn't want to invade his privacy but she had to know something about him. She debated whether she should Google him to find out something that she could talk to him about.

Nervously typing, his name came up. Shelby paid the service to help her do some undercover work. She didn't have time to read everything that the computer system had found. Instead, she just printed every page and planned to read it later.

Kingston

Kingston walked back to his room to grab his keys, wallet and phone. He had very little time to waste. He let Tiana know that he would be back in a little while. He had some business to handle. He was done playing their games; he didn't want his dangerous side to come out. If that was what they wanted it to be, then he would grant them their wish.

Jaxson crossed the line when he put his hands on Tiana, even though he was trying his best to act like a tough guy. It didn't fit his true character. He was the family snitch; Jaxson was the type to call the cops. All talk but no bark.

Virginia pretended to be the good Samaritan, but loved to talk shit about people behind their backs. She was the devil's mistress. She cleaned out their mother's bank account. How could a child steal from their own mother? This was before LillyMae died of cancer.

Chyna only cared about getting high and using people for whatever she could get her greedy hands on. She had control over her children. LillyMae did most of her parenting for her.

The only sibling Kingston had that treated him like a brother was Chase, before he got killed by a drunk driver. Kingston missed his brother.

Just a few minutes away from Virginia's house, Kingston felt his phone vibrate in his pocket. He ignored the call, knowing it wasn't important. He was not in the mood to talk to anyone; he was still angry. LillyMae worked so hard to love and care for her children, and those who claimed to love her did her dirty. The more Kingston thought about how they all mistreated her, the angrier he was getting. He pulled over to an abandoned gas station.

Kingston was on the verge of crying. He wanted his beloved mother and brother back. He would sell his soul to the devil if it meant bringing them back. He missed both of their funerals on account of being in prison. His phone vibrated again. He took it out and it was Shelby.

"Girl what is it? Damn, you really enjoy stalking the shit out of me," Kingston snapped.

"I apologize; it's just that I really like you. I thought maybe when you come back to Colorado to visit that I could take you out and get to know each other. It seems to me that you are not ready to talk to me on that level. Whenever you are, just give me a call. I won't bother you anymore."

Kingston didn't mean to go off on her. He just needed some space with everything going on with Rene and everything else. It wasn't her fault. Taking a deep breath, Kingston apologized to Shelby. He promised her that he would call her. He just had a lot of business to take care of and family problems to solve. Once he got that squared away then they could have a proper conversation. He was just having a stressful day.

Kingston felt better after he apologized to Shelby. He knew LillyMae would be disappointed if he didn't make things right. He was human; he was entitled to make mistakes. This was not like him to take his anger out on another person. He could lighten up spend a few hours with her. What was the harm?

"I'll tell you what: when I come out that way again, I will take you out for some ice cream. We can even go for a walk in the park," Kingston suggested.

"I would love that; it's a date when I see you." Shelby laughed.

"Yeah I guess it is a date. I will call you when I get a chance. Once again, I apologize for my outburst; you didn't deserve that."

Kingston was shocked that he had made a date. He never thought in a million years that he would ask a woman out. Looking toward the sky as the sun was shining, Kingston shielded his eyes as he smiled. He knew who to thank for this.

"Thanks Mom; I love you."

Chapter 18

Elizabeth

Elizabeth redialed her friend's number; this was an emergency. She needed her help to win Sam back.

"Come on bitch; I know you see me calling. Don't make me add you to my list of kills," Elizabeth mumbled.

Pacing back and forth, Elizabeth wondered why her friend wasn't answering her calls. Was Sam fucking another white girl behind Rene's back?

If so, Elizabeth would kill them both. Or maybe just the new mistress chick who was trying to take Sam away from her. She tried one more time before her friend answered the phone. By the tone of her voice, Elizabeth can tell she wasn't happy to hear from her.

"What the fuck do you want, Elizabeth?" Shelby yelled.

"Is that the way to answer your phone? Didn't your mother teach you any manners?" Elizabeth asked.

"Look, I am very busy. The last time I heard from your bitch ass, it damn near cost me my job and medical license."

"That was then and this is now. I suggest that you stop acting like miss goody two shoes. We both know your ass is far from perfect. The only reason I changed my statement was because I knew that you would be a valuable asset to me."

"What in the hell do you want with me, bitch?"

"I need you to help me pull off a pregnancy," Elizabeth stated.

Shelby fell silent for a few moments before she spoke again. "You want to repeat what you just said?"

"I said I need your help to pull off a pregnancy."

"Have you lost your damn mind? There is no way in the hell that I am going to help you pull off a fake pregnancy. I know it will be fake because you can't have any more children. Whose relationship are you trying to destroy now?"

Elizabeth didn't want to explain. It was none of Shelby's fucking business. She didn't need the third degree. If she was to tell her why, Shelby would only try to talk her out of it.

"Let's just say that it's someone I really love and care about. I never dreamed that I would catch feelings for this guy. He's retired from the army. He is a sexy black chocolate man that I can't stop thinking about. Leah needs a father in her life."

Shelby tried to redirect. "Elizabeth, is this guy already taken, and since when did you start to like black men?"

"Since the first day I saw him. It's none of your business. You are half black and white, so what difference does it make? If black women knew how to treat black men, they wouldn't leave them and come to us."

"Excuse me? This is not a racial debate, so don't you dare say that to me ever again. Just because you got some black dick up your white ass doesn't mean that you are a black woman. Yes, I am half black, but I never used any racial comments toward them or any race. Back to my original question; is this man taken or not?"

"Fine; yes he is married to a complete bitch that doesn't deserve him. Today I went by their house and that brat of a son of theirs screamed at me. She came out and starting punching and hitting me. Someone called the cops and I drove off."

"This man is married with a family, Elizabeth! Have you stopped taking your meds? If so, you need to get back on them. If this guy cheated on his wife and she finds out about it, they could end up in divorce court and you don't want to be responsible for breaking up a happy home. Chances are this guy will not divorce his wife to be with you. I will not take any part in helping you destroy that man's life."

Elizabeth persisted. "Yes, you will, or I will tell everyone your dark secret that I have kept for many years. Remember I have the power to destroy your career and life. You masterminded the entire operation. The only reason the old gang hasn't come after you is because you paid them a nice check to keep quiet. We did our time while you continued to save lives, pretending nothing ever happened."

Shelby was quiet for a moment. "I will need time to think about this before I make a decision. Who is this guy we are talking about?"

"His name is Sam Smith. He is married to a woman named Rene, and she is destroying his life while I am trying to save him and be a family together."

Shelby

Shelby spit the cool water out of her mouth. She couldn't believe Elizabeth. Shelby knew Rene! She delivered her baby. Kingston was Rene's uncle; the man who promised to take her out for ice cream and go to the park.

How could she play both sides of the field without getting caught up in real life drama?

If Kingston ever found out what she did many years ago or that she helped destroyed his family, he would never forgive her. Looking at her printer to retrieve those papers that she had printed earlier, she briefly read over what she had found. She needed to dig a little deeper.

She needed to know everything about Kingston and his family. Shelby had never been in this situation before. She really liked Kingston. How could she choose between the man that she was falling for her and her dark secret that Elizabeth was holding over her head?

Rene

I tried my best to put on a happy face battling my feelings toward Sam. I couldn't shake the nagging feeling that he was lying to me. If Sam never slept with Elizabeth, why the crazy obsession?

"Mom, you haven't gotten up to eat anything. You love coming here. I know it's none of my business, but are you trying another crash diet or something?" Junior asked.

I snapped out of it and look at my son with a smile. It was time to put Elizabeth out of my mind and focus on my family. This was our weekend together. I couldn't let my personal feelings get in the way. It wasn't fair to Junior. I would have to wait until Monday to deal with crazy ass Elizabeth.

"You're right; I was trying a new diet. but this food is so tempting. I just couldn't figure out if I should cheat on it or not. Don't pay any attention to me - why don't you go on up and fix your plate and see if any of my favorites are up there? Then I will sneak up there to cheat for a day."

Junior smiled back at me and got up.

Kingston

Kingston was glad he got things squared away with Shelby. He continued his journey to Virginia's house, changing his mind about leaving a calling card. He would make himself seen to let them know not to fuck with him.

Kingston blamed his siblings for the death of LillyMae. She never would have gotten cancer and died if they all would have taken care of her the way she did them. Or at least kept her alive until he was released from prison.

Just as he was about to pull up, Chyna drove past him and pulled up into Virginia's driveway, parking her car next to Jaxson's truck. Moments later, Raymond pulled up and parked on the other side of their house. Kingston parked on the other side of the street.

Turning off the engine putting on his dark shades, Kingston got out and locked his doors. He walked briskly toward Virginia's house, excited about seeing his so-called siblings. This would be a family reunion that they would never forget. Before he made his presence known, he would scope out the place.

Kingston knew how to pick locks. During his check out, he saw they had decided to get another guard dog. The dog was on the other side of the house, sleeping. Looking inside the window, Kingston could hear Virginia discussing him with the others. They all were trying to get Jaxson to call the cops and press charges. Jaxson kept repeating that he was not going to do that.

"Of course, he's not, because he knows that if I went to jail and Tiana found out, she would bail me out and tell the cops that he grabbed her and I was protecting her. She could press charges against him," Kingston said to himself.

Listening for a few more minutes, Kingston decided it was time to come out of the darkness. Slowly and quietly raising the window, he climbed inside. In his mind, Michael Jackson wasn't the only smooth criminal.

While they were busy talking and babying Jaxson, they didn't notice that Kingston was standing right there, looking and flashing his famous smile. Kingston was wondering how long it was going to take for them to notice that there was an elephant in the room. Virginia suggested that they buy a gun in case Kingston tried to come and attack. They would shoot him dead.

Kingston laughed to make his presence known, slowly pulling off his shades and tucking them into his pocket. Everyone was startled; they didn't know how he got in. They didn't even hear him coming. He could see how frightened Virginia looked as she eased her way toward Raymond.

"Well, isn't this lovely? I'm sure mother would have been pleased that all her children have managed to come together in one place. Let me just say this before I continue: Jaxson, why don't you tell them the real reason why your drunk, police-calling ass got whipped. Let me help you out: nobody puts their hands on my baby girl! Fucking with Tiana will get you killed."

Everyone remained silent as Kingston continued.

"Now that we have cleared that up, let's move on, shall we? You all been wondering about who I intend to harm next." Kingston looked at Virginia. "If you think about plotting against me for any reason, I will come back and cut each and every one of you up and feed you to the garbage disposal. It's bad enough that none of you wanted to take care of our mother, which is why she left me and Tiana. Shame on you Virginia, that you stole everything from her. She gave you life and that's how you repaid her."

Virginia looked stunned, but Kingston was nowhere near finished.

"You all could have helped mother. I don't want to hear it, because it will be lies anyway. Now that you all have seen me, you can stop wondering. Raymond, I have no problem with you. From what my mother shared with me, at least you tried to pay her back."

Raymond didn't respond.

"Let me smarten you up a little bit though; it wasn't your debt to pay back! It was your bitch's debt," Kingston bellowed.

"Mother forgave me for that, and I don't know why it matters to you," Virginia interrupted.

"You haven't been forgiven by me, you evil selfish bitch!" Kingston barked.

He turned to Chyna. "Chyna, you are a fucking nurse. Why couldn't you take care of her? She raised your damn children. All you do is think about yourself, drugs and these deadbeat ass niggas that can't do shit for you. Then you wonder why your children have no respect for you."

He went to Jaxson next.

"Jaxson, I will not stand here and allow you to disrespect my mother again. I should have stopped your ass a long time ago. All you care about is Gina's white ass and she don't give two fucks about you."

No one said anything for a moment. They were all too nervous to speak. Then Kingston took another look at Chyna.

"This bastard put his hands on your daughter, and you over here stitching him up. You should slap his ass -

oh wait, I already did that for you. No need to thank me. I have said my peace. With that, you may all carry on with your day."

Kingston took his shades back out of his pocket and walked past Jaxson, opening the front door to leave. They all rushed to the window to see if he was really gone. Chyna and Virginia checked the house to make sure he didn't steal anything. They discovered how he got into their house when they saw the open window.

Chapter 19

Shelby

Shelby was going to take the rest of the day off after hearing Elizabeth's plans to break up another marriage. She needed to go home and have a drink.

Rene and Tiana had been nothing but sweet and kind to her. She couldn't betray their friendship.

Collecting her things and letting the other staff members know she wasn't feeling well, Shelby left. She had to put a stop to the madness. She couldn't tell Rene and Sam about what Elizabeth's plan was. If she did, Shelby could get in serious trouble. If Elizabeth got caught, then Leah could end up in the state's custody.

Shelby knew talking Elizabeth out of it would be a waste of time. She really needed to hear Kingston's voice even though she decided to give him his space. She could try to tip him off, but that would only add to what he was already going through.

Taking a chance, she called him anyway. Even if it went to voicemail, as long that she could hear his voice, she would settle for that. To her surprise, he answered and didn't sound upset.

"Hello pretty lady," Kingston answered.

"Hi, sexy man. I forgot to mention that my favorite ice cream is butter pecan. When you come out to visit me you will know what to order." Shelby smiled.

"Is that the only reason you called?" Kingston asked.

"Honestly, I was thinking about you and how much I am really missing you. I just can't stop thinking about you. It's been such a long time since I have found myself attracted to any man."

Kingston

Kingston couldn't believe that he was hearing this. From where he come from, the man told a woman how he felt and let her take the lead. In his mind, times had really changed.

"Wow, I can't believe you told me reasons behind these calls and text messages. I am flattered that you feel that way about me. No woman has never said those words to me. Forgive me if I am taken by surprise." Kingston laughed. "How was your day at work?"

"It was hectic but enjoyable. I'm headed home now to relax. I am going to order some dinner since I don't feel like cooking."

"All that fast food isn't good for your health, but since you declared that you had a hectic day you deserve to treat yourself to something special."

"Yeah, I am really looking forward to seeing you. I know that you are a very busy man so I will not take much more of your time. If you see Tiana, tell her I said hi and you both take care. Enjoy your weekend."

"I sure will, pretty lady. I am looking forward to seeing you too. How about we add a meal to that ice cream date?"

"It's a date that I am really getting excited about!"

They laughed and chatted for a few more minutes before hanging up. Shelby was happy to make the phone call. She had a date with the sexiest man in the world. She decided that she really needed to take better care of herself. She didn't want another woman trying to steal

Kingston away from her. She could handle a long-distance relationship.

There was nothing that could spoil her happy mood. Shelby felt like she was floating on cloud nine. She would find a way to stop this madness and keep her secret from making headlines.

If Elizabeth thought she could bully her, then she really didn't know Shelby at all. Shelby's mind flashed back to Kingston. Hearing him call her pretty lady sent butterflies to her stomach.

Driving home, she could see Elizabeth's car parked in her driveway. Didn't they just talk over the phone? Shelby circled back around. She didn't want to be spotted when she left. She decided to call in tomorrow just in case Elizabeth came to her job looking for her. Shelby turned on her house alarm through her phone. After today, she would set it just to feel safe.

"Dammit Elizabeth! You will not ruin that family's life just because you got the hots for someone else's husband."

Shelby's phone buzzed with a text from Kingston.

I have never been on a date. I have no favorite ice cream, but I will stop by the store to try that butter pecan. I had a nice time talking to you. Enjoy your weekend pretty lady.

"Lord, that man gives me goosebumps no matter what he does or says. As long that he's willing to give me a chance, I will be the happiest woman in the world." Shelby giggled.

Rene

I watched as everyone had a good time talking and laughing. I wasn't on no diet. I was happy being a full-figured woman. Sam used to make me feel special; not anymore.

I could tell Sam was staring at me, smiling. I didn't know why; there was no way he was going to talk me into letting him stay in the same room tonight.

"Baby, I am sorry that I went to Elizabeth's house without you, but she needed to hear it from me that she will not hurt you or try to destroy our happy home. I don't like to see you sad. I know I am the reason why you have those sad puppy eyes. From now on things are going to change," Sam said.

He took my hands in his and kissed them as he held them tight and firm. I wanted so badly to believe that things would change between us. I wanted my marriage to work. Maybe we could go to a marriage counselor. I was a damn good wife and mother. What I couldn't understand was why Sam constantly cheated on me? I never cheated on him. I had plenty of chances too.

Two wrongs didn't make a right.

I wanted to pull my hand away. The way he held it was just the same he held it on our first date. We gazed into each other's eyes. I tried to fight back the tear that was beginning to slide down my face. Sam wiped it a way gently.

Sam got up and led me to the buffet. I let him take the lead for once. I would definitely be calling Tiana soon. I needed some serious advice. I couldn't fall for Sam's lies again.

Sam

I knew Rene was going into heat. I wanted her as much as she wanted me. For the moment, I would have to control myself.

We filled our plates to rejoin Junior at the table. I leaned down and kissed her, taking her breath away. I was praying that it would change her mind. We looked at Junior, who was smiling. We owed it to him; he needed both of his parents, not just one.

Rene

My stomach was growling, so I dug in, not sure what to expect after Sam kissed me. It had been a long time since I blushed like that in public, feeling like a teenager. Sam and Junior were both smiling at me. If I could only shake that feeling about Sam, then everything would be okay. Billy taught me never to ignore my basic instincts; always trust my gut.

Sam picked up his fork and started to eat.

"Hey, I was wondering if it would be alright if I spent the night at Jose's?" Junior chimed in.

"It's okay with me if it's okay with your mom," Sam replied.

"Sure, you can," I said.

I finally felt myself relax for a brief moment. Sam and Junior were talking about sports. I suggested we go bowling after we leave to give me a chance to work off some of the extra pounds that I packed on with this meal.

We spotted Shelby walking in to place her order as we left.

"Hey Shelby, how are you"? I asked.

"Hi, I am fine. Thought I'd get my dinner to go, working crazy hours at the hospital. Your uncle Kingston and I have a date when he comes out to visit. I am so happy! I should go shopping and pick out a new outfit. I want to look perfect for him," Shelby explained.

Sam and Junior exchanged hellos with Shelby.

Sam invited Shelby to come bowling with us. That way, I would have a bowling partner. Shelby hesitated, then agreed.

"I would love to come and have some fun for a change. I must warn you though: I am not the best bowler. It's been ages since the last time I went," Shelby explained.

"Neither is Rene, so you two will be perfect partners." Sam laughed.

Chapter 20

Shelby

Taking a few deep breaths before getting out of the car, Shelby hoped the owners of the bowling alley did not recognize her. It was a long time ago; she just wanted to forget about it. The last time she had been here, her late husband Larry had slapped her for causing them to lose and poured a pitcher of beer over her head. Now that she was parked outside, Shelby wasn't sure if this was such a good idea.

Sam gently knocked on her window, asking if she was going to get out. Shelby gave him a slight smile before opening her door.

Sam helped her out of her car while Rene and Junior waited for them to catch up.

"Hey, you alright? You seem nervous," Rene asked.

Shelby nodded. "Yeah I am fine. This place brought back a painful memory for me. Nothing to worry about. We came to have fun and we will. It's not every day that I get out and mingle."

"I can understand that; just relax for a few hours and you can tell me about your date that you and uncle Kingston are planning. Maybe I can help you shop for something pretty," Rene suggested.

Shelby smiled. That would be good idea; then she could pick Rene's brains about a woman trying to sabotage her marriage.

"I would love that! Maybe we can shop tomorrow if you are not busy. As you can see, I don't have many friends that would like to go shopping with me or have lunch."

Rene didn't respond to Shelby's comment.

"Hey, are you two coming? I am ready to win. Junior and I don't have all day," Sam joked.

"Yes, we are coming. Hold your horses. We will catch up in a moment. While you're in there, get some drinks and snacks just in case you get hungry again," Rene announced.

Shelby could tell Sam loved his family. Elizabeth was trying her best to steal their joy and happiness. She prayed that she would one day have that same feeling with Kingston.

"You have such a lovely family. No matter what you do, always love and cherish them," Shelby said to Rene through tearful eyes.

Rene stared at her.

"Shelby, I don't know where that statement came from, but I do appreciate it very much. However, there is only one person who thinks differently about my family, and that's this woman named Elizabeth."

Just hearing Elizabeth's name made Shelby gasp. She decided not to ask about Elizabeth because she didn't want Rene to pick up that she knew her.

She wanted to tell Rene Elizabeth's fake pregnancy plan, but it would ruin her friendship with Kingston.

"Shelby, are you sure that you are alright? I am starting to worry about you," Rene asked.

"I'm fine. I was making a comment that shouldn't have been said in the first place. No need to worry about me. I love seeing happy, loving, families."

Rene

I didn't believe what Shelby said. I didn't press the issue either, but I decided just to watch out for her.

Whatever secret she was hiding would soon come to light. As soon as I mentioned Elizabeth's name, Shelby got shook.

"Okay, is everyone ready to get their bowl on? I know I am ready show you people who the real master is," Sam said with excitement.

"Oh, you got big balls. I might not have been the best bowler, but I can hold my own. The only way I had lost that last night was because you came up from behind me and tickled me." I laughed.

"I might do it again." Sam winked at me.

"I hate to interrupt but that is consider cheating," Shelby proclaimed.

"Can we please start the game? I do have other plans," Junior complained.

"I will go first; that way everyone can watch the master." Sam chuckled.

Picking up his ball to roll it down the lane, Sam landed his first strike. Then Junior took his turn. He knocked down a few pins, giving Sam a high five. Then it was my turn. I got a gutter ball. Shelby took her turn and got a strike.

"Wow, you got a strike! maybe you can give my wife a few pointers. Judging from the first try, I can feel some competition coming on," Sam jabbered.

"Well, we can have a nice friendly bet. I don't mind taking your lunch money," Shelby crooned.

"I got a hundred bucks that says that I am still the bowling champion," Sam boasted.

"Great; you're on. Dude I can't wait to take your lunch money."

I would have gotten involved in the bet, but I wanted to see how poor of a bowler Shelby really was. From what I observed so far, Shelby wasn't as bad she let on. Everyone was having a nice time Sam and Shelby talked trash to one another as they bowled.

I could feel my mixed emotions starting to take over again. No matter how hard I tried to ignore the fact, something was wrong. I wondered if there was a connection between Sam and Shelby. Although Shelby seemed smitten with Kingston, I decided I would give him a call to see how he felt about her.

"Come on Rene! Get your head back into the game. I really want to take your husband's lunch money," Shelby joked.

I wondered if Shelby was a drinker. I picked up my ball to take my turn. I thought about suggesting we go out for drinks after we went shopping for her outfit; make it a girl's day out. Too bad Tiana wasn't around to help me fish for the information that I needed.

Rolling the ball down the lane, I made a strike. While the others were cheering, I just turned around and took a bow. Smiling to myself, I walked over to Shelby to exchange high fives with her.

"Hey, what do you say tomorrow we make it a girl's day out. We can even have a couple of drinks."

"Sure, I would love that. As soon as I take your husband's lunch money. It will be a trip on him." Shelby giggled.

Returning the laughter, I was shocked that Shelby took the bait. Continuing with the game, everyone was down for the last count. The winner would take all. I couldn't wait to get it over with. I was ready to go, but I knew how competitive Sam could be and Junior was having a great time.

Raymond

"I can't believe that he just broke into my house and started talking shit and have the nerve to threaten us!" Virginia yelled.

"You didn't tell me that you were at my daughter's house showing your ass, and my grandson was there. Have you lost your drunk ass mind?" Chyna shouted at Jaxson.

"Alright everybody; let's all calm down," Raymond advised.

"Jaxson, why did you go over there in the first place, considering your relationship with Tiana? She doesn't want to breath the same air as you," Raymond asked.

Everyone looked at Jaxson, waiting for an answer. He looked at Virginia before speaking.

"Virginia called me and told me what had happened between them. I went to her house to get some answers. I knew Tiana was holding information since Kingston was her favorite uncle. She would go to war when it comes to him. We all know that Kingston was our mother's favorite child. Even though she loved all of us, she loved Kingston more," Jaxson confessed.

Raymond looked at Virginia. He knew she was the reason they had a fight. She just had to open her mouth and start trouble. He always told her to stay out of people's business. He would speak to her about it later. For now, he wanted to know why Jaxson put his hands on Tiana. There was so much bad blood in the family, he didn't know where to begin.

Years ago, when Chase was killed by a drunk driver, LillyMae sued and won plenty of money. No one knew how much she won. She trusted Virginia to help her put it in a bank. Virginia was secretly stealing money out of the bank account. The bank tried hard to get LillyMae to press charges. The whole family had turned their backs on Virginia. Raymond went to LillyMae crying his eyes out. He just couldn't lose his wife. He would pay back the money she had taken.

Six months went by and Raymond never missed a payment. LillyMae was grateful. When Raymond went to make another payment LillyMae, told him to "stop bringing her money". She said she prayed about it and put Virginia in God's hands. Raymond felt terrible.

"Jaxson, continue the story. After you got off the phone with Virginia, you went over to Tiana's looking for Kingston to cause trouble, didn't you?" Raymond accused.

Jaxson just stared at him.

"Well Jaxson, am I right or wrong? Just because you had a talk with Virginia doesn't mean that you can go over there looking for trouble," Raymond scolded. "Chyna if you are done patching Jaxson up, I would like to have a word with my wife. You go check on Tiana to make sure she is okay. Gives you a chance to see your grandson."

China agreed, and Jaxson stood to leave.

Chyna

Gathering her things to leave, Chyna wanted to slap Jaxson and curse out Virginia. Her daughter was none of Virginia's business. She had Raymond Junior to think about. That boy was thirty-three years old and still lived at home with his parents. Raymond tried to move out a few times, but Virginia guilt tripped his ass into moving back in.

Chyna's mind shifted to Tiana and Kingston. In Tiana eyes, nobody could come close to her heart like Kingston.

He had been her favorite uncle since she was born. She didn't want nobody to touch her but him. Chyna often felt jealous of the relationship that Kingston and Tiana shared. The only reason Tiana and Chyna had a fallen out because Tiana felt Chyna was never around, only coming to her whenever she was in need of money.

Tiana labeled Chyna as a bad parent. She really hated the ground that Willie, her father, walked on. Chyna still remembered the ass whooping that Kingston gave to him when he spanked her and left a bruise.

Virginia

Virginia knew once they left, all hell was going to break loose. Raymond was going to lose his temper. No one had never seen how mad Raymond could really get. It took a lot to make him lose his temper. He was the kind of man who liked to live in peace, always lending a shoulder to cry on. He wasn't into violence, but he was getting sick and tired of cleaning up Virginia's bullshit.

Waiting for them to leave, Virginia thought about how she could talk her way out of this one. She wasn't expecting for Jaxson to throw her under the bus. This was not her fault. If Tiana would have been honest from the start, nobody would have gotten hurt. Raymond looked out the window to make sure the coast was clear since Raymond Junior was out with Dexter and Sara Jean. It would be hours before he returned.

"What have I always told you about sticking your big nose where it doesn't belong?" Raymond barked. "I have had it up to here with this business meddling of yours! You go out and start trouble and a bunch of unnecessary mess for me to clean up. When will you ever learn to mind your own damn business?"

Raymond went down the hallway to change out of his chef's uniform, still mumbling underneath his breath. While he was in his room changing, Virginia took that as her opportunity to get away; she left.

Chapter 21

Elizabeth

Elizabeth got the feeling that Shelby was trying her best to avoid her. There was no way she would be working this late. She'd called Shelby several times and gotten her voicemail. Shelby was also not answering her texts. Elizabeth checked her job as well and they told her Shelby left hours ago. Where in the hell could she have gone to?

Driving past Sam's house, Elizabeth saw that the only vehicle parked in the driveway was Rene's. Elizabeth had a gut feeling that Shelby believed she would not expose her for not helping with the pregnancy scam.

Losing her patience, she knew Leah was hungry. Elizabeth needed to stop somewhere to get dinner.

"Dammit Shelby; where are you?" Elizabeth bellowed.

Deciding on getting pizza, Leah's favorite, she would try to make it a fun Saturday. Elizabeth needed to keep her mind on something positive until she got a hold of Shelby. Calling her phone again once again, she got Shelby's voicemail. Already feeling like pulling out her hair and screaming, Elizabeth stopped herself. She didn't want to frighten Leah.

Trying to force the tears to stop coming down her face, Elizabeth quickly wiped them. Leah had saw the sad look on her mother's face. She was a smart three-year-old.

"Mommy, what's wrong"? Leah asked.

"I'm fine; just the wind is blowing in Mommy's eyes. Nothing is wrong. Why don't you finish reading your book or play with one of your toys tonight? We can have your favorite, pizza!"

Seeing Leah's smile that could light up a Christmas tree made Elizabeth feel better, but she needed some time alone. She wondered if her friend Janet was available. She always loved to babysit Leah.

Elizabeth took out her phone once more to call Janet, hoping that it would be a yes. Janet picked up after several rings, sounding out of breath.

"Hey Janet! I was wondering if you would like to babysit Leah for me?" Elizabeth asked.

"Uh, tonight is not a good night. Any other night it would be yes. I have special plans this weekend that I can't break. I'm sorry, tell Leah I said hi," Janet replied.

Janet disconnected the call before Elizabeth had a chance to plead her case. Elizabeth wanted to scream. This was important. She was on a mission that had to be completed. It was only for one night. Since she didn't have a plan B, Shelby got lucky this time. But she hadn't seen the last of Elizabeth; not by a long shot.

Shelby

Shelby was praying like hell that Elizabeth would be gone by the time she made it back home. Still deciding on how to tell Rene and Sam about the fake pregnancy, the more she thought about it, the more she dreaded the idea of having to be the bearer of bad news.

Shelby felt bad for Leah. What would happened to her if her mom went back to prison? Who would want the sweet little girl? How could Elizabeth be so selfish? There were so many free single men out there in the world that would love her and Leah, but no, she would choose a man that was already married with a family of his own.

Even though Shelby was getting close to her mid-fifties, she would love to be a mother. Since breast cancer robbed her of that chance, she would never know how it would feel.

Babysitting Leah a few times brought some special joy into her life. She was a darling angel every time Shelby looked at her. Leah reminded her of Pebbles Flintstone with her flaming red hair and beautiful dark eyes. An idea hit Shelby on how this plan might work, if she could get Rene and Sam's help. She would love to adopt Leah. Even if Kingston didn't want to be more than friends, at least she would have Leah to love.

Shaking off her thoughts, it was time to get back to the game. Since Larry wasn't here to embarrass her in front of everyone, she could win and take Sam's money. Already down to the last frame, it was all or nothing. Shelby prayed that she would win. She was able to keep up with Sam. They had been neck and neck for a while. Shelby planned to text Kingston to let him know she made it home and spent the evening with Rene and her family.

Picking up her ball and getting set to roll it down the lane, Sam and Junior chanted, trying to mess up her concentration. It was time to show them who was the real master at bowling. Really, Shelby wasn't as bad as she claimed to be. She just told people that because she lost interest. Spending this fun evening with Rene, Sam, and Junior was the best time of her life.

As the ball was rolling down the lane scoring a strike, Shelby jumped up and down, screaming her head off. Everyone turned around to see what the commotion was about. Sam took out his wallet to pay the money while challenging her to a rematch. Shelby gladly accepted his challenge. Looking at the time, she knew she better get home. They might have other plans. Giving everyone a hug before she left, she hoped like hell she didn't run into Elizabeth.

Rene

"Wow! You took that loss like a champ. Usually you would keep going and going until you had won." I laughed.

"Yeah it's on. We do have a rematch coming up. That will give me time to practice. She snuck that last strike on me. It's cool though; I won the real grand prize right here," Sam replied.

He grabbed me and pulled me close for another kiss. I didn't know why I let him do this to me. It was great spending time together as a family; however, it didn't justify Sam's actions or the secret that he was keeping from me. I still felt we should sleep in separate bedrooms. I slowly backed away from Sam's embrace before I caved.

"Let's get the snacks packed up so Junior can get his overnight bag ready. It's been a fun evening; I really did enjoy myself."

"I did too; I can't wait to tell Jose about it," Junior agreed.

"We need to do this more often. I am the one to blame about this. Things are going to change for the better. I promise we are going to make time to do more family activities," Sam stated.

Shelby

Driving home, Shelby turned on her favorite radio station to take the edge off. That was the most fun she'd had in years. She was looking forward to her rematch with Sam. Going out for drinks with Rene was also a nice suggestion. Shelby could see the love that Sam had for his wife. Elizabeth didn't stand a chance with him. Thankful to not see Elizabeth still waiting for her in the driveway, Shelby opened the garage, pulling in and closing it behind her.

The more she stayed out of sight, the better.

Sam

Getting everything packed and making sure to clean up the mess, I wondered if Rene had changed her mind about sleeping in separate bedrooms. I would try again once I got Junior packed for the overnight stay at Jose's. I wasn't about to go down without a fight. I was lucky Rene allowed me to touch her and sneak in a couple of kisses.

"It looks like we got everything cleaned up and packed now; let's get going so Junior can have his night of fun at Jose's house and then we can have our night of fun." I grinned at my wife.

Rene

I was in the mood for sexual healing, but I knew what Sam's motives were. I couldn't let my guard down. I had to fight hard against his temptation; there was no way he was getting off the hook. I prayed a silent prayer to myself. He grabbed my hand. Still feeling his magical touch, I repeated over again in my mind, *Do not give in.*

Junior

Unlocking the car door for his mother and waiting for her to get in, Junior was getting restless. He just wanted to go over to Jose's house since Jose didn't live too far from Elizabeth. Junior planned to give her a piece of his mind. He would have Jose secretly record it, just in case she tried to lie her way out of it.

He had to help save his parents' marriage. After he made his voice heard, he would get back to his uncles. His had to give his dad credit; he really was trying to make his mom happy again. At first Junior was upset with how that he had treated them, but after today's family fun, he could forgive his father. Junior knew not to stick his nose into grown folks' business. He also wanted to talk to his dad about Elizabeth. Since Shelby and Rene would be gone all day Sunday, they could have a heart-to-heart talk then.

Chapter 22

Shelby

Shelby thanked God that she made it home safely without Elizabeth stalking her. She needed to take a few days off from work to get things sorted out. She sent Kingston a quick text before she got settled in for the rest of the night. The fact that he replied sent shivers down her spine.

Shelby filled up her bathtub, adding her favorite cherry blossom bubble bath while still smiling. She didn't want to think about anyone but Kingston. She walked into the kitchen to reheat her dinner she had purchased at Golden Corral. Her phone started to ring. It was Elizabeth calling her. She hit the Ignore button.

"I am not talking to you, Elizabeth! If anyone is going to lose in the end, it will be you. I will not let you destroy that man's family or my friendship with Kingston, you miserable ass bitch!" Shelby screamed.

Taking a deep breath, she remembered the papers she had in her bag about Kingston and wondered if she should still call her friend to dig deeper and find more information about him. Until she made her final decision, she would read what she had first.

She went back into her bathroom to turn off the water, wishing Kingston was with her at that very moment. She wouldn't mind sharing a bath or a shower with him.

She heard her phone ring and let the answering machine do its job. It was Elizabeth leaving her a message. Instead of just Sunday, Shelby would email her boss, letting him know that she needed some personal time off.

Taking off her work clothes and sliding into the tub, Shelby could feel the tension leaving her body immediately. Resting her head back against the wall and closing her eyes, she let the soothing sensation take over. Peace and quiet was what she needed right now. No drama, no sick patients, or having her name called a million times over the intercom.

The microwave beeped, letting her know her food was ready but Shelby didn't move. The bath felt so good. Slowly opening her eyes, she grabbed her sponge and washed her body. She wished it was Kingston washing her body. The more she thought about him and their upcoming date, the more excited she got. Taking another few minutes before she got out, Shelby leaned back against the wall, thinking about her date with Rene tomorrow.

Feeling the water getting cold, she pulled the plug to drain the water, then stood. She grabbed her towel as she stepped out, drying herself off. She went into her bedroom to grab a night shirt and panties.

Sitting on the bed, she lotioned herself with cocoa butter. She dressed in her panties and night shirt. She walked into the kitchen to retrieve her food.

Shelby turned on the TV to watch the local news, then changed channels to watch an action movie. Taking the papers out of her briefcase to read about Kingston, she couldn't remember where she left off that made her gasp. Not really paying much attention to the movie, she was more focused on what she was learning about him.

Elizabeth

Elizabeth couldn't believe Shelby was really testing her patience. She would make good on her promise. If Shelby didn't help with her plan to get Sam away from Rene, Elizabeth would drag her name through the mud. Calling her house and cell phone repeatedly, Elizabeth knew that she had to be home by now.

It was too late to get Leah ready to make the long drive back to her house. If she could find someone to watch her for an hour or so, it would be great. Elizabeth didn't trust a lot of people with her daughter. The only ones she trusted were Rene before their friendship came to an end, Janet, her neighbor, and Shelby because she was a medical doctor.

Shelby avoiding her at all costs was a very bad decision. Elizabeth wasn't the type to be ignored. Whatever Shelby was planning, Elizabeth was ready for it.

Rene

I was staring out the window as Sam drove home. The temptation was too hard for me to fight off. I blamed Sam for this. He knew my weak spots. I silently cursed myself out for letting him get to me. I had been a few months since I had sex. My body was craving it.

I tried my best to ignore the sexual healing calling, then R. Kelly's "Bump & Grind" song popped into my head.

I was a huge fan of his. I knew those women were trying to destroy his music career. The more I thought about him, I didn't realize that Sam was running his hand on the side of my left thigh, sending electric shocks. I grabbed his hand to place it back on his thigh. My pussy was burning. He knew he was sparking all kinds of flames that I couldn't resist. I glanced at Sam, who was smiling. He knew he had me right where he wanted me.

Sam

Tonight, I was going to prove how much I really loved her. No more having affairs. All the women I had ever been with, Rene was only one who truly stuck by my side.

I was truly grateful for that. Any other woman would have left me high and dry. Rene was different: she was strong, loving, caring, a hard worker. I knew I made the right decision when I married her. I had to think how to make this night more magical while Junior was spending the night at Jose's. I couldn't afford to make another mistake. I wanted to be the one to put the stars back into her eyes.

After pulling into our driveway, I got out and walked around to the other side of the car to open her door. She took my hand as I gently helped her out of the car. Junior raced up to the door and ran upstairs.

Junior rushed back down the stairs almost out of breath. Rene and I looked at one another. We knew Junior and Jose couldn't wait to play video games and talk trash to each other. I offered to drop Junior off, then I would be back with a couple of surprises of my own.

Rene

I wondered what Sam was up to. While he was out, I checked my messages. I really needed to call Tiana. This would be the only time that I could talk freely.

I walked into the living room and grabbed the house phone to dial Tiana's number. I hoped I wasn't calling too late. Tiana answered as I kicked off my shoes.

"Hello family," I said.

"Hi, what a surprise to hear your voice," Tiana replied.

"Girl, I have so much to tell you. I have no clue where to begin."

"Start from the beginning and go from there."

Once I got the ball rolling, I didn't stop until I got everything off my chest.

Tiana

Tiana was shocked and stunned all at once. The way that Rene was sounding, Tiana knew she needed her help. Nobody messed with her cousin. Rene was more of a sister than Sara Jean was. She was always available for Tiana whenever she needed her.

Tiana scribbled the name *Elizabeth Waters* on a note pad. She would be looking into her past. She had to know everything about this woman, if she was this bad of a person that Rene was making her out to be.

Tiana had told Rene about the fight between Kingston and Jaxson. Rene said she couldn't believe it. She knew Jaxson had it coming. He always had a way to push another person's buttons. Never in a million years did she think it would have been Kingston's buttons that got pushed.

Before they ended the call, Rene invited her and Genesis to come out to Colorado to visit them.

Sam

I dropped off Junior at Jose's house, thankful that me and Rene had the place all to ourselves. Just the thought of pulling her into my arms to make passionate love was driving me crazy. I had to be slick like Barry

White, Marvin Gaye, Michael Jackson, and Prince. I had to set the mood, take my time, plan it just right.

Junior

Once Junior got inside his friend's house, he told Jose that he felt Elizabeth was trying to break up his parents. He had to stop her before anything bad happened. Jose was a few inches taller than Junior. He had black spiked hair and black glasses. They were more like brothers than best friends. Jose was ten pounds heavier than Junior. Jose had an older sister who always picked on him; Stella was cute and adorable. Brown hair and eyes, she was graduating from high school soon. Their mother was a sweet lady. Joanne was a nurse.

Jose seemed excited to get into mischief with Junior. The boys decided to wait until Stella went into her room so they could sneak out together.

Chapter 23

Shelby

Shelby was reading what she had found out about Kingston from the internet. Serving thirty years in prison mostly for burglary, having an unregistered weapon, etcetera. Shelby wasn't one to judge though; she was no saint either. She had done some hurtful things herself.

Looking at his picture, Shelby knew they would make a beautiful couple. Their ten-year age difference didn't faze her. All she cared about was that Kingston gave her a chance to love him. She wished she could have gotten to know his mother before she passed; then she could fill her in on how to keep her son happy. That would be a great topic that she could talk to him about: his mother.

Shelby's father Harold was a proud black man who was working in a factory for many years. He met her mother Betty who was a white woman; the daughter of John, the Governor of Colorado. In those days, blacks and whites weren't allowed to mix like they were in today's world.

Betty's family was extremely racist; the only person they didn't treat harshly was her nanny, Lucille. Shelby adored Lucille more than she did her own mother. Lucille was six-foot-four and weighed three hundred pounds. She spoke her mind freely and did her job. It only took one time for Betty's father John to call Lucille a nigger, and before anyone could intervene, John was seeing stars, the moon, and the little bird that says tweet. Lucille was the type of woman who played by her own rules and demanded her respect.

Harold was delivering milk to their home as a second job to earn some extra money. When Harold met Betty, it was love at first sight. Like the old saying goes, once you go black you can't go back. Betty was hooked. Lucille was the one who always told her mother if they were going to be a couple, they had to keep it a secret. She came from money and power; he didn't. Betty, the stubborn person she always had been, ignored her. No matter how many times Lucille tried to warn her, there was no way she was going to keep her relationship a secret.

Betty and Harold ran off and got married. When the news hit the streets, everyone in the family went out of their way to make Harold's life a living hell. Later on, Betty got tired of being a wife and mother. She met another guy while Harold was working two jobs. That was when she had Elizabeth, who she put up for adoption, then went back to her husband and Shelby.

Elizabeth and Shelby didn't know they were half-sisters until they had a DNA test done. Elizabeth never knew the love of a family. She was bounced around from foster home to foster home. She always blamed Shelby for having a loving family with two parents who loved her very much.

Shelby's life was hell on earth, however. Her grandmother Dorothy was the reason. She always referred to Shelby as half nigger baby, half and half, or even the family mistake. Not letting it stop her, Shelby had to work twice as hard to prove she was just as qualified as anyone else in the world.

Elizabeth only wanted to bring shame into their family to expose their mother's secret to the world. Not only that, Elizabeth also knew that Shelby was having an affair with the warden where Elizabeth was serving her prison sentence. In order to keep Elizabeth's mouth shut, Shelby paid Elizabeth. Shelby and the warden were caught red-handed. When Elizabeth was supposed to be cleaning, she didn't bother to knock; she just barged in while they were in the middle of having sex. He was also having sex with a few other inmates. Ayden was the type of warden you couldn't threaten; he would make your life a living hell.

A few inmates had gotten pregnant by him. He would sneak them down to Shelby's office and force them to have abortions. Ayden's wife couldn't have children of her own. Someone from the other side leaked information to his wife, Samantha. She hired a private investigator to confirm her suspicion of Ayden's infidelity. A few months later, he was fired. Samantha took everything he had.

Elizabeth threatened to tell Samantha about Ayden's affair with Shelby. Shelby called her bluff. Samantha didn't care; she had already ruined Ayden's life. He couldn't get a job working in law enforcement. The biggest regret Shelby had was when the state released Elizabeth. She invited her to move to Colorado and start a new life. By the time she had arrived, Elizabeth already had Leah.

Thinking they could rekindle their friendship and become sisters turned out to be the biggest mistake Shelby ever made. Elizabeth was a user and liar. It didn't matter to her whose happiness she destroyed, as long as she got what she wanted out of the deal. Shelby confided in Elizabeth about when she was in medical school. She was raped by her college professor. When she reported him to the school's administration and medical board without any witnesses, her case was dismissed.

A few years later, he was diagnosed with heart disease. Any little thing that upset him might have killed him. He was involved in a car crash and placed on life support. Elizabeth at the time was working at the hospital as a housekeeper. Shelby didn't think that anyone would be watching when she slipped into his room to turn off his machine. Standing there watching him take his last breath, she turned back on the machine, slipping out of his room before the nurses and doctors came running in.

Elizabeth confronted her about what she did and said that for the right price, she would keep her mouth shut. Shelby didn't take to kindly to anyone threatening her. That was when Shelby had enough of Elizabeth. It was time to get rid of her. She went to Aaron, who was the supervisor of housekeeping and very fond of Shelby. Elizabeth was fired immediately.

Elizabeth had no idea that Shelby was the reason she lost her job. Not having contact with her mother Betty, Shelby knew that the only person who could answer her questions about Elizabeth was her father, whoever the hell he might be.

Shelby continued to read Kingston's history. He was a teenager when these crimes were committed; how could the state of Oklahoma treat him that way? The more she read about him, the more fascinated with him she became.

Shelby also looked into adoption for Leah. She already had it set in her mind that she would create her own family, even if Kingston felt he didn't want to be with her.

It was time to send Elizabeth back to prison. This time, she would be spending the rest of her life there, with no chance for parole. Shelby would not be a part of her scheme to destroy that poor man's family. Until she talked to Sam and Rene, Shelby would keep a low profile and stay far away from Elizabeth.

Junior

Looking at their watches, Jose and Junior were wondering when Stella would be going into her room. Junior was becoming more eager by the minute. Trying to kill some time, they decided to talk about sports: the one thing Stella couldn't stand.

Once Jose got the conversation started, Junior smiled. Stella rolled her eyes and got up. She locked her room door behind her.

Junior and Jose quietly opened the door to the back patio, hoping Stella wouldn't hear them. They heard her blasting music from her room, so they knew they were safe for the moment. Jose tossed Junior a helmet for safety and hopped on the bike with Junior behind him. They took off on Stella's motor bike, heading to Elizabeth house.

Junior was hoping to catch her at home alone. He had some things that he really needed to get off his chest. There was no way he was going to stand by and do nothing. He wished Jose would drive this bike a little faster. Junior also wished that he had some money he could have a taxi or an Uber take him to Elizabeth's house.

"Jose will you please drive this bike? I want to get this over with. We don't have much time before Stella comes out of her room and discovers her bike is missing."

"It will be hours before she comes out; she is blasting music and probably looking at Drake pictures on the internet while talking to her nerdy friends. Relax, we got plenty of time; besides, we are almost there."

Junior's stomach was doing flip flops. Maybe Elizabeth would call his parents and tell on him. He would be in big trouble if she did.

Parking Stella's bike next to Elizabeth's car, Jose was checking it out. He loved cars more than he loved sports. Junior tapped him on his shoulder to remind him they were here on business, not car shopping.

"Get the phone out and get ready to record," Junior said.

Jose gave Junior the thumbs up and turned the camera on, but kept it out of sight. Junior rang the doorbell. They could hear Leah yelling inside. Elizabeth opened the door, looking surprised to see Junior.

"Hey guys, would you like to come in?" Elizabeth greeted.

Neither of them said a word until they were inside.

Junior started. "Elizabeth, I want you to stay away from my dad. He is married to my mom and they love each other. There is no way that he will leave us to come be with you and Leah. This is my family that you are playing games with. I have no idea why you and my mom are not friends anymore and I really could care less. You mess with my mom again and make her very mad like you did today, and you will be forced to deal with me."

Elizabeth looked shocked, but Junior went on.

"Elizabeth, you are toxic waste. I feel sorry that Leah has a mom who's a loser. My dad doesn't love you and never will. The sooner that you realize that, the better. I am telling you to stay away from my parents," Junior warned.

Elizabeth

Elizabeth didn't know rather to smack the shit out of this kid or shoot him. Lucky for Junior, he was only a kid. She would notify Sam about how he came to her house and was being rude and disrespectful to her in her own home. She knew how to make things very dramatic.

Elizabeth finally spoke. "Now you listen to me: first of all, I will not stay away from Sam. Your mother is just being paranoid about my relationship with your father. Oops, I meant my friendship with him. And second, you really need to mind your own business kid. If your father wants to stop seeing me then he will. Your mother and my friendship came to an ending because she wanted it to end. I have been nothing but nice to your mom. She is the one who needs medical help for her paranoia. Now that I have listened to you and your story, it's time for you and little friend to leave. One more thing: if you ever come to my house again without me inviting you over, it will be hell to pay," Elizabeth threatened.

Junior

Junior balled up his fists. He really wanted to black out Elizabeth's eye. Lucky for her, he didn't hit girls, no matter how much they made him mad. And his parents would not be too pleased about it either.

"Elizabeth, you don't scare me. You have no idea what kind of family I come from. I am the one who you don't want to make enemies with. Go ahead and call my parents. I know that you are itching to call my dad and rat me out," Junior said.

"Come on buddy let's go; you made your point." Jose slapped Junior on the back.

As the boys were leaving, Junior whispered to Jose, "Did you get all of that on video?"

Chapter 24

Sam

I stopped by the flower shop to purchase some red roses and candy; next stop was the liquor store to purchase some Arbor Mist wine: Rene's favorite. It had been a long time since I saw Rene dressed in something sexy. I decided to go to Walmart, where I saw lingerie with a matching robe that I thought would look amazing on Rene.

I couldn't wait to purchase the items. Feeling good, I was hoping that Rene would be willing to let me light the fire that I placed inside her body.

My phone rang and I ignored it, keeping my eyes on the road. I was on a mission tonight. I had a sweet sexy chocolate mama at home waiting for me. Junior was fine at his sleepover.

My phone rang again in the Walmart parking lot. Once I pulled inside a space, I took my phone out and saw it was Elizabeth. "What will it take to get you to stop calling me?" I yelled. Her number was getting blocked after this call.

"Junior and his friend Jose came to my home. Junior was cursing at me, calling me bitches and whores, telling me that I am a loser and I can kiss his ass and suck his dick. I can't believe he would disrespect me like that!" Elizabeth cried out.

I listened as she continued.

"When I asked them to leave, he said if I called you or Rene that he would come back and beat the hell out of me and have Jose's dogs demolish Leah." Elizabeth sobbed in my ear.

"Elizabeth, do you really think I would believe that cock bullshit story that you are trying to feed me?" I sneered. "My son doesn't talk that way. Rene and I didn't rise him that way and you know it. I can't believe that you said that shit to me. Stop calling me and stay away. I have no interest in you; never have and never will. I am not divorcing Rene to be with you. I am not attracted to white women. It was only a fantasy; nothing more."

"Sam, please don't say that to me. What we have is special. It's real. You were starting to fall for me. You were catching real feelings until Rene interrupted us. I know that you want me as much as I need you, and Leah needs you too. We all can be a happy family. I will not leave you Sam, no matter what you say to me. I will do anything for you to keep you in our lives. I gave my heart to you. Leah loves you like you are her father; you can't walk out on us now!"

I hung up the phone and blocked Elizabeth's number.

Shelby

Shelby could feel her eyes getting heavy. Tomorrow would be a better day. She dreamed about Kingston. She often wondered if he thought about her as much as thought about him. She didn't want to seem pushy, but she was getting older. It was time for her to settle down. After Larry died, she remained single and celibate until she found the right man to marry. Saying a silent prayer, she really wanted to know more about Kingston.

Since she had a shopping and drink day with Rene, maybe she could see if Rene would help shed some light on her uncle. That would make her date with Kingston more interesting. Just thinking about him brought a smile to her face.

Junior

Jose told Junior that he knew how painful it was not to have two parents living in the same house. His dad was in prison. His mom worked a lot, and soon, Stella would be graduating from high school and moving out.

The boys flattened two of Elizabeth's tires after she closed the door. Thankfully, her alarm didn't go off. They knew Elizabeth didn't lock her car doors. It was easy for Junior to get in and pop open the front hood to do more damage. After they were finished, Jose turned to Junior.

"Let's get out of here before Stella comes out of her room."

Getting on the bike to head home, Junior was glad that he brought Jose along to record their meeting. Junior knew Elizabeth wanted to break his parents up. What he couldn't figure out was why? He wanted to say more, but he also knew they didn't have a lot of time. He just prayed that Stella stayed in her room a while longer until they got back. Lord knew she would have a fit if she found out they took her bike.

Rene

I was glad I called Tiana to vent. There was so much I wanted to get off my chest. Now I was wondering if my marriage was worth fighting for? I fought so many times to make it work by giving Sam everything that he needed. Now I wanted a divorce or just to separate until I could figure out what I really wanted to do.

Tiana advised me to wait until they come out to visit so we could find out more about Elizabeth and Sam's affair together.

No matter how many times I asked Sam, it was the same damn answer. Just thinking about it was making me mad. If I couldn't get the truth from Sam, what would it hurt to ask the nasty white bitch her side of the story? I took out my phone and dialed Elizabeth's number. Tiana would be upset at me for not waiting for her to come. Elizabeth answered.

"Elizabeth, I got some serious questions that you need to answer. I want the truth: is there something going on between you and Sam?"

Elizabeth sounded like she couldn't wait to spill the beans. "Let me just say this to you, and after this, don't call me anymore. It's bad enough that son of yours came over with his little friend and disrespected me in my home. Now you want to know if your husband is stepping out on you again. To answer your question, he has been mighty happy when he does come to see me. What you can't nor won't do for him, his white snow bunny will. Now you figure it out since you're the educated black woman. I am just a dumb ass white girl with a child to raise with the help of government assistance."

I hung up in her face. That bitch was really trying my patience, which was not a good thing for her. Now she was lying about Junior and Jose coming to her home?

I decided to forget about Elizabeth for now. "Tiana was right; that bitch would say anything just to keep trouble started."

I went into the kitchen to pour myself a glass of wine. It was time to find out all about Elizabeth Waters. There was something very sneaky about her that didn't sit right with me. Sam nor Elizabeth were willing to be honest with me. I was sick and tired of playing this little game with them.

I slowly drank my wine. This was what I needed. Just thinking about Sam sleeping with Elizabeth made me sick to my stomach. I wanted to believe that they didn't have sex, but if they didn't have sex, why would Elizabeth make it seem that they had?

I refilled my glass and drank some more, wishing I didn't make that phone call after all.

I decided to make another phone call, to my uncle Billy.

"Hello baby," Billy answered in his sweet voice.

"Hi uncle; I need your help with Elizabeth Waters. I need you to gather as much information on her as possible. She wants a war. Sam is going to file a protective order against her on Monday. He wants me to file one on her as well. She came to my house. I ended up putting my hands on her."

"Are you hurt?" Billy asked with concern.

"No, I am fine. I just want her to go away and stay from Sam. I'm trying to get him to tell me the truth about his friendship with her, but he keeps giving me the same old bullshit answer."

Billy

Billy wasn't liking the sound of this story. It was time to make an appearance. He was already on the case to find out about this Elizabeth person when he was on the phone talking to Junior hours before. Junior still hadn't gotten back to him. Billy wondered if he got back in touch with Kingston?

"I will see what I can do. In the meantime, I need you to put away your boxing gloves. We don't have any proof of what has occurred between them. From what you told me, she sounds like she is jealous of you."

Billy would call Sam's no good sneaky ass again. Listening to Rene talk about her incident only made him hate Sam even more.

"Listen to me; I will do whatever I can to help you solve this problem, but I have to agree with Sam. You need to file a protective order against her. Who knows what she is capable of? Until I know what we are up against, I need you to keep your distance. Block her number as well from all social media accounts. Don't let her stress you out under no circumstance. You got my great nephew to take care of."

Rene

I knew he was right, but I wasn't no punk; you come for me and I would come back at you with everything I had. This wasn't my first rodeo. I went through the same kind of hell with Rachel. It took her years before she got defeated and now it was Elizabeth's turn to suffer the same fate that she did.

Next time I would try to put a handle on my anger. I couldn't let a thirsty ass bitch make me come out of character. It was bad enough that black women got talked down on and disrespected because they couldn't control their actions or behavior. There was more than one way to skin a rabbit.

"Okay Uncle. I will try my best not to let that ugly snowman looking white bitch make me come out of my comfort zone." I smiled.

Billy

Billy didn't know that Elizabeth was white until Rene mentioned it. There was no way in hell Sam would cheat on Rene with a white woman. Then he thought about Sam and Rachel; she was Hispanic. Sam would stick his dick into anything as long she had female body parts. Billy couldn't wait to face off with him. The more he thought about all of his affairs, the more he wanted to end Sam's life. He knew how much Rene and Junior loved his sorry ass though.

Billy searched Elizabeth's name on Facebook.

He decided to create a fake profile and send her a request. That way, he could get the real story from her. Billy was taught that women gossip more than chickens who share a chicken shack.

Rene

Disconnecting the call, I was thankful I had family I could depend on when times got rough and dark. Tiana taught me that if you can't depend on family then who can you depend on? I got a taste for some ice cream. I decided to call Sam and have him stop at a store on his way back home. He should have been back by now.

"Hello beautiful," he answered. "I am at Walmart shopping. I know I am running late. Did you need anything before I come home? It's my fault; I didn't mean to come in here and take so long. I just had some ideas to go with your surprise that I wanted to create for you."

I felt stupid for giving him an ounce of trust or decency. I was confused. Why did it have to take for me to threaten to leave him in order to get him to act like the husband I had fallen in love with years ago?

"I just wanted some ice cream. That's what I was calling for. You can take your time and shop. I am about to go upstairs and shower, then watch some TV.".

"No! baby please wait until I come home and yeah, I will bring you back some ice cream. Is there anything else you want me to grab?"

"I guess I can wait a little while longer to see what kind of surprise that you got for me. It wouldn't hurt for me to wonder what you are up to."

"Thanks, beautiful. I will see you soon. Love you so much."

Just hearing him say those words would have meant the world to me before. Now, they didn't have that same effect. I didn't want to say it back and give him false hope.

"I will see you when you get here."

I hung up and wanted to cry my eyes out. Why was this devil bitch trying to destroy my marriage, happiness, and family?

Chapter 25

Junior

Jose and Junior made it back in time to park Stella's bike before she came out of her room. Not sure what their next move should be, Junior was certain that after they had left Elizabeth's house she would call his parents. Junior prayed that he didn't get Jose into trouble. It was his idea. Junior would take all the blame if it was brought to his mom's attention.

Stella came out of her room and saw them outside.

She came outside with glasses of lemonade.

"Hey guys, why are you staring into outer space?" Stella asked.

"We are just looking. I am surprised that you actually came out of your room to see if we were still alive; we could have been abducted by aliens," Jose commented.

Junior didn't say anything he just watched. He took a sip of his lemonade as he continued to watch Jose and Stella's conversation. It was entertainment to him.

Jose and Stella went back and forth for a few moments.

"Hey guys; how long is the argument going to last?" Junior asked.

"Oh, sorry buddy. As you can see, Stella has a way of pushing my buttons. She is very annoying," Jose replied.

Stella rolled her eyes and walked back into the house.

Jose turned to Junior when his sister was safely inside. "Tell me, do you really believe that Elizabeth will call your parents? If she does, that makes her a snitching rat."

"She can tell them if she wants to. I said what I needed to say. Now I got to wait and see if she will take my warning seriously," Junior replied.

Taking a snack off the tray that Stella had brought out, they both went back to looking at the sky.

Billy

Billy used the alias Olivia Winter. He sent out a few friend requests to random people just in case Elizabeth decided to check out the description. He scrolled down to see if she had mutual friends.

Carefully looking, Billy wanted to make sure that he had the right person. He ran across Rene's name as her mutual friend. Clicking on her profile, Billy saw that Elizabeth was Sam's friend as well.

"Bingo; now I got you bitch. And what the fuck did Sam see that is so attractive about you?" Billy asked himself.

Billy sent her a friend request. Just to sweeten the pot, he also sent one out to Rene, Sam, and Shelby. He remembered the first time he met Shelby. She was remarkably beautiful. But she wanted Kingston instead.

It hurt for a while. Billy wasn't so sure if Kingston was attracted to her as much as Shelby was to him. He was never the one to compete with any man over a woman though. If she wanted to talk to him, that would be her move. Billy was done chasing women. He would speak to them. If they wanted more, he would simply let them take the lead.

Waiting for Elizabeth to reply to his response to get the ball rolling, he knew she was the right chicken head to spill the tea. He wondered how much tea she would be willing to spill. If she told him that they had sex, that would be the end of Sam's life. That had always been one of Billy's pet peeves; don't lie to him or make a promise that you can't keep.

Logging onto Facebook messenger, Billy wondered if Elizabeth was online. She wasn't. There was still time for her to accept his request. If not, he had more ways to connect with her. She couldn't escape from him no matter how hard she tried. Just as he was about to resort to plan B, he saw that Elizabeth had accepted his friend request. Billy smiled to himself. Now it was time to get into character.

He felt like a kid in a candy store, starting with small talk. Elizabeth hopped on messenger to finish more of their friendly conversation. He knew he had to take baby steps. He didn't want to give anything away that would make her suspicious of him; then he would be in trouble.

Elizabeth

Elizabeth couldn't believe that Sam didn't buy her story. She tried to make it as dramatic as possible. Now Rene wanted to know about their love affair. Elizabeth smiled. She enjoyed playing with Rene's mind.

She was glad that Rene did call her. It served her right for putting her hands on her. She couldn't just come out and say yes, they had been fucking for a long time and she had no plans of stopping now. She would save that part of her story until Shelby helped her pull off the fake pregnancy scam. If Sam wasn't willing to come back to her, then she would force him to come back to her.

Elizabeth accepted Olivia Winter's request. It seemed that she knew Sam, Rene, and Shelby. She wondered how they knew each other. From their small talk, it seemed like Olivia was a sweet person who liked to have fun. Talking a look at her pictures, Elizabeth saw that she was cute. She couldn't have been no more than twenty-five years old.

Reading her profile, Elizabeth was intrigued by Olivia. She could invite her out to Colorado to hang out with her.

Sam

After leaving Walmart, I decided to go check on Junior to make sure that everything was okay. If there was a chance Elizabeth told the truth about him and Jose stopping by her house, I didn't want my son involved.

Elizabeth

Elizabeth tried calling Shelby once more before she headed off to bed. Leah was already sleeping. Elizabeth was so happy that she kept her. Leah was the only person who loved her unconditionally. All she needed was a father figure in her life. If only Rene would just file for a divorce and never come back. Dialing Shelby number, Elizabeth knew she was at home by now; she wouldn't be out this late. Just as she was about to hang up, she heard a sleepy Shelby answer the phone.

"Hello."

"It's about time you answered the fucking phone. Bitch, I came by your house and waited, then I called your job. They said that you left hours ago. I've been trying to get a hold of you to discuss our business arrangement, or else I will have to expose you to the media, the medical board, and that poor man's family that you killed, not to mention the whole state of Colorado will know exactly who your relatives are. I will bring down the entire clan."

Shelby

Shelby sat up in bed, turning on her night lamp on. She was in a peaceful sleep, dreaming about Kingston and the paradise they would share together. She should have checked her caller id before she answered the phone. Hearing Elizabeth throw a baby tantrum was not a good look for her. Shelby had enough of it.

"Elizabeth, I am grown ass woman. I can come and go any time I damn well please. First of all, we didn't have a business arrangement to discuss. That man is married with a family of his own. Secondly, my family doesn't owe you a damn thing. You drag them into this and they will fuck up your world. Third, I don't take kindly to being threatened. I haven't made up my mind yet. You will not rush me into helping you destroy a happy marriage. Why don't you grow up and be a mom to Leah and stop worrying about another woman's husband? You want a man so bad? Get a newspaper and pick one out of the Classified's."

Slamming down her before phone before Elizabeth could reply, Shelby decided she would tell Rene and Sam everything. Elizabeth was getting out of control. She had to be stopped before someone got hurt.

Sam

I pulled up on the side of the curb where Junior and Jose were shooting basketball, having a grand old time. As soon as I saw that, I knew Elizabeth had lied. I smiled, pulling off. My son was fine. Now it was time to go home and save my marriage.

I parked next to Rene, getting the bags out of the car, rolling up the window, and turning on the car alarm. It was time to win Rene back. Rene was on the couch watching *Golden Girls*. I kissed her forehead.

I made my way upstairs to lay out the new lingerie on the bed, then went to the bathroom to fill up the tub adding bubbles. I placed the chocolate candy on a breakfast tray, along with the rest of the goodies.

Rene

I wondered what in the world he was doing, so I got up from my spot, sneaking upstairs. I peeked around the corner and saw Sam busying himself in the bedroom, walking from the bathroom to the bedroom. Looking at the new lingerie he had placed on our bed, I smiled. I turned around and snuck back downstairs, pretending I doesn't know what he was up to.

"Damn him; he is making this hard for me to keep him at a distance. I really want to keep up this brick wall. He has to be punished. I know there is more to this story."

That sexual itch was coming back. One night of passion wouldn't hurt.

Chapter 26

Kingston

Kingston couldn't stop thinking about Shelby. He wondered if it was okay to call her. He finally decided he wanted to have a special lady in his life. He originally thought he had that chance with Rebecca, but after she had taken him for granted, he never trusted another woman again.

Kingston went through his closet to see what he should pack for his upcoming trip. He would get Tiana to help him shop. That was one of her favorite hobbies. Just seeing the looks on Jaxson and Virginia's faces was priceless. Before he left, he wanted to take a trip to LillyMae's grave. It had been a long time since he brought her some fresh flowers.

Kingston wished she had fought a little longer until he released from prison. He would have taken care of her; never would have left her side. If he didn't commit those crimes, he wouldn't been sentenced to thirty years. Thankfully, she never abandoned him when he needed her the most. He was a kid trying to be the man of the house. LillyMae was the kind of mother who would work and sometimes went without as long her children were taken care of.

He tried not to let her memory bother him. He would go visit his mother and bring her fresh flowers. They would chat like old times. He didn't get the chance to protect her from those assholes who stressed her out so bad until she was laying in her casket. He vowed to protect Tiana from them; he would be damned if they hurt his niece. She was the only one who had been there for him since the day she was born.

Stopping by Best Yet flower shop to get LillyMae some fresh roses, Kingston wondered if she would have liked Shelby as she liked Elizabeth, who was her nurse at the time she was receiving her cancer treatments. Now he'd met Shelby who was a doctor. Smiling to himself, Kingston figured it was a sign he should date a woman who was in the medical profession.

Kingston selected the red roses. He knew that LillyMae loved all kinds of flowers, but he wanted her to have roses. Every time she smiled, it reminded him of roses. Even when Tiana smiled, it reminded him of roses. He paid for the flowers, then headed off to the gravesite to spend time with his mother.

Driving up to her grave, Kingston could feel the tears starting to swell up. He knew men weren't supposed to cry, but he really missed the only woman who made him feel special. Getting out of the car, he took the flowers and placed them on her grave. He stooped down, touching her headstone, not sure where to even begin. He rubbed his hands back and forth, trying his best to contain his anger that was beginning to take over him.

"You were not supposed to leave me, Mother. I don't know how I am going to make it without you. Not having you here is so painful. Tiana has been an amazing blessing in my life, and so has Genesis. They are the reason I keep going. I wish that I could hear your voice again. I would sell my soul to the devil just to have you back," Kingston cried out.

"I even made a date with this lady named Shelby. I'm not sure if I am ready to date again or fully commit myself to a woman after what happened between me and

Rebecca. I just don't believe that I can trust again. I liked Elizabeth the nurse that went out of her way to look after you while you were in the hospital, but I didn't want a relationship while I was in prison. Honestly mother, I just don't know how to love again. I agreed to go out on a date with Shelby though. Guess I could allow myself to have some fun. I know that Tiana is grown up with a child of her own, but I feel they need me a lot more than Shelby does. The funny thing is, I can't stop thinking about her. I know she means well. Today I kind of blew up at her for no reason. I did apologize though. It wasn't her fault. She didn't deserve that, but I made things right with her. Well mother, I better go. Continue to rest with the angels. I love you."

He took one last look before walking away. Kingston didn't know what kind of feeling he was having when it came to Shelby. He knew he was too old to be having a crush on someone who he only met once and talked to over the phone for the last few years. Maybe he should find out more about her first. He didn't want to pry into her private life though. So far, she hadn't given him any reason to investigate her. Getting hungry, Kingston knew he better return home before Tiana filed him missing.

Sam

I was busy getting everything ready for this date night with Rene. I couldn't fail her again. This was my one and only chance to prove to her that I meant everything I said. Actions spoke louder than words. It was time to get back to being Captain Romance again. I took a step back to admire my handiwork. The bathroom was decorated with scented candles, a bubble bath with rose petals, a breakfast stand filled with chocolate candies and fruit, and music playing our favorite love songs. I smiled to myself, then went back into the bathroom. I found Rene's favorite lotion that she purchased from Bath and Body Works. Now it was time to surprise her. I walked back downstairs.

"My beautiful lady, may I have this chance to be your servant tonight?" I asked.

Rene

I stood, wanting to stay mad at him. I couldn't let Sam break me down, play with my mind or heart again. I tried my best not to look into his chocolate brown eyes or that Morris Chestnut smile.

He took my hands into his as he kissed both of them. Picking me up and kissing me again, he knew that would drive me out of my mind. He carried me up the stairs and into the bathroom, putting me down.

I tried not to let the beautiful scene tear down my brick wall.

I internally cursed myself for allowing Sam to touch me. My body tensed as my heart raced. I wasn't sure what to do next. My mind told me to run out, but my heart said to stay with him and let him love me the way I needed to be loved.

Sam wrapped his arms around me, kissing me on the neck. "I love you," he whispered in my ear, sending shivers down my body. Having these mixed emotions, I closed my eyes, squeezing them tightly shut. I didn't want to have tears falling down my face. The more I tried to fight it, I was failing.

I slowly opened my eyes and Sam looked at me through the mirror. I knew he saw the pain and hurt he caused her. He turned me around and softly kissed each tear away.

He began undressing me, kissing me more passionately. Hungry for more, I stripped his clothes off too.

Sam

Skipping the bath for now, I wanted to feel her ride me off into the sunset. I kissed each one of her breasts. Hearing Rene moan as she spread her legs apart made me want to taste her so bad. I took my time as I licked her, sucking on her pearl bud. Rene was screaming my name over and over again. She belonged to me now and forever. If I was lucky, tonight Junior might have a sibling on the way.

"Oh baby give it to me; you so tight and taste so good." I moaned, then rose up, looking at Rene's angelic face. I felt my dick get hard. As I slipped it inside Rene's love tunnel, I was ready to get down to business. I pushed every one of my nine inches inside her walls. Rene dug her nails into my back, arching hers. I switched positions. I didn't mind that she took all her frustration out on me sexually. She could punish me all night with sexual pleasures.

"Aw Rene, that's it! Punish your dick, baby. Take it all. You're the only woman I want. You can't leave me; you're mine for life!" I yelled.

Having hours of sexual encounters, we both were breathless. I pulled her into my arms and kissed the top of her head.

Rene

As we lay there on the floor, I didn't say anything. I could feel his heartbeat. I was surprised that his heartbeat matched mine. Yet I still wondered why he would cheat on me. If not with Elizabeth, then with who?

Lifting my head up, I got up to check the temperature in the bathtub. Sam must have made the water scolding hot. He knew he was going to make love to me at some point. The water was just right. I did love hot baths, but not too hot. The water had cooled down some.

Sam got up and helped me in the tub, then he followed behind me. We both sat and he pulled me into his chest. He washed my body, taking his time massaging my breasts, then making his way down between my legs.

"Baby, what we have is a real. Our marriage is real. We have years of history. There is no way you are leaving me. I made some horrible mistakes, but this is my way of winning you back into my life. I can't afford to lose you. I wouldn't be able to survive without you," Sam confessed.

I was speechless. I didn't know to respond to that. Just listening to Aaron Hall sing made me dream about making love to him.

Chapter 27

Elizabeth

Elizabeth was furious. She didn't expect Shelby to talk to her that way. Elizabeth had done her homework on Shelby's life. She knew more about her than what she shared. Shelby wouldn't want to Elizabeth make good on her threats, because Elizabeth could and would her destroy her life.

All she asked was that Shelby help her get the man of her dreams; the man she loved with all her heart. Elizabeth wasn't asking her to go out and rob banks. She just wanted Sam; nothing more. She was forced to give up one man that she loved before; giving up Sam wouldn't be fair. Why couldn't she be loved by someone other than Leah, or deserve a man who wanted a family and treated her like Sam had in the past?

"Damn you, Rene! You don't need a man like Sam to love you the way he was loving me," Elizabeth screamed at her walls. "You evil bitch! I hate you with all my heart. You just couldn't stand to see me happy with Sam or Leah to have a father figure. You are a selfish bitch. I hope you rot in hell. I can't wait to send you there. I am going to kill you."

Wiping the tears from her eyes, Elizabeth was sick of going to bed with no man to hold her. Why did Rene get to have the perfect family, or Shelby to get to have a successful career and a family who loved her?

Elizabeth looked in the mirror, trying to find the answers to her questions. She was heavy-set with straight brown hair, wore glasses, and was just a plain Jane. No makeup. Elizabeth felt like an ugly duckling. How could she be good to fuck in the bedroom but not good enough to be a real man's special woman?

She thought back to her childhood and how she was given up for adoption, getting bounced from foster home to foster home until she was eighteen years old. Nobody wanted her. She often thought about committing suicide, feeling unworthy of love. But if she died, who would raise Leah?

Hearing her phone ring, Elizabeth raced to answer it. She was hoping it was Sam, but it was Janet calling her.

"Hello, I am sorry I couldn't watch Leah for you. I just felt horrible," Janet said.

"It's fine; no need to explain it to me. I should have asked you ahead of time."

"You sound horrible; have you been crying?" Janet asked with concern.

"I'm fine; you don't need to worry about me."

"I'm coming over. I will bring a bottle of wine and snacks. I feel like you need to talk. I know it's getting late, but I just can't leave things the way they are."

Elizabeth sighed. "If you want to stop by, fine, but Leah is asleep. Just to give you a fair warning."

"It's fine darling. I am just so worried about you. I was being a selfish friend. Let me make it up to you."

"I will see you when you get here."

Elizabeth went to wash her face. She knew she looked horrible. She didn't want to scare off Janet. Janet might be the one who would understand her and see things from her side.

Rene

The water was getting cold. I stood, ready to dry off and get ready for bed. I wasn't in the mood to eat any of the delicious treats Sam had prepared for me. Sam got out as well, letting the water run out.

He helped me dry off. I reached for my toothbrush to brush my teeth before I drifted off to sleep. Sam continued to watch me as he did the same. He walked her over to the bed taking the lotion to massage my body. I could hear him moan while he applied it to my curves. I was starting to feel the fire once again. I fought the sensation. Sam brought the lingerie over to me, and I had to admit that he had good taste. It felt good to wear something sexy to bed for once. Sam grinned as he watched me getting dressed for bed.

We climbed into bed and I wanted him to go to sleep in the guest bedroom, but I didn't want to hurt his feelings. Sam slid over next to me, putting his arm around me and kissing me good night. He whispered, "I love you." I didn't say anything. I just let the sleep claim my body.

Kingston

Going to visit LillyMae's grave did Kingston a world of good. It was not the same as seeing her in person, but he tried to remember the good times they shared. He dialed Shelby's number, hoping to catch her before she called it a night.

"Hello," Shelby answered.

"Hello pretty lady, I was hoping to catch you before you went to bed," Kingston proclaimed.

"No, I am up. I guess I must have dozed off. I spent the evening with Rene and her family, bowling.

Tomorrow she and I are going to go shopping and have a drink afterward. I took a few days off from work. I need the rest to chill out."

Kingston was enjoying the way she ranted on and on. Maybe he needed to move on with his life. He knew Rebecca had left him forever, taking their two sons. All he could do was pray that God would reunite them.

"I am glad that you had a good time tonight. With all the hours you have been working, you do need a break to take care of yourself."

"How was your day today?" Shelby asked.

"The same as always; same shit on a different day. Nothing special. I just left from visiting my mothers' grave. Brought her some fresh roses and now I am headed home before Tiana files me missing." Kingston laughed.

"I wish I could have met your mother. She seemed like she was a loving and beautiful woman."

"She was my world. I wish that you could have met her too." Kingston smiled.

"When you come out to visit me, bring pictures of her. I would love to see her, then you can tell me all about her," Shelby suggested.

"I will bring some of the ones that I got left. I could talk about my mother all day long but I'm not going to bore you with the stories. You can tell me something of you and your family. I would love to see pictures of them as well."

"I would love that. Gives us a chance to get to know each other better over ice cream." Shelby laughed.

Kingston loved the little giggle laughs Shelby did. It reminded him of the way a baby laughed.

"Well pretty lady, I will say good night, and have fun with Rene tomorrow." Kingston smiled.

"Good night. Thanks for the call; I can get a good night sleep now that I had a chance to talk to you."

Hanging up, Kingston was still smiling. He was just a few miles away from Tiana's house. He didn't mean to be gone so long. Now he had a date with a doctor. He hoped she would accept his past. Most women believed that once a person went to prison, they should be judged, before they even knew your story or reason. Shelby didn't seem like the person who would judge him for the mistakes he made.

Not every woman wanted to hear about a man's dead mother. From the conversation he was having with Shelby, she seemed very interested. He couldn't wait to get to know more about her.

Pulling up to Tiana's driveway, he got out and unlocked the door. Genesis was sound asleep in his play pen. Tiana was busy on her computer. From what he could see, she was doing some research on Elizabeth Waters. It wasn't the Elizabeth the nurse, was it? He would ask about that later. He went to go fix his dinner plate.

The food Tiana cooked smelled good. She really outdid herself the way LillyMae would do when she cooked homemade food. He couldn't wait to eat; he was starving. Looking into the fridge to grab a soda, he took his plate back into the living room to sit down to eat. Tiana was so busy on her computer that she didn't notice when he came in.

Tiana

Trying to find as much information about Elizabeth that she could to help Rene with was damn near impossible. Tiana would try social media later. She knew hacking was against the law, but if Rene was planning to take Elizabeth down, she was going to need all the ammo she could get to destroy her once and for all.

Kingston

Looking at Genesis sleeping away, Kingston was proud of Tiana for raising him as a single parent, not letting anything or anyone stop her from reaching her dreams and goals. Savoring the food, he got up to refill his plate, taking advantage of Tiana's cooking. He wondered if Shelby could cook?

"Save some room for dessert!" Tiana yelled.

Kingston wondered what she made for dessert. Looking in the freezer, he saw ice cream and popsicles. Closing it, he reopened the fridge and saw that Tiana made her famous banana pudding and peach cobbler. He shook his head. She was definitely LillyMae's granddaughter. Closing the fridge, he decided he would get some after he showered and got ready for bed. Walking back into the living room to retrieve his spot on the sofa, Tiana finished typing, taking a break to turn around and face her favorite uncle.

"Well you certainly have been gone a while; what's her name?" Tiana commented.

"You are the only woman in my life. I went to Virginia's house and made my presence known and voice heard. Left there and went to visit my mother. I even put fresh roses on her grave. Talked to Shelby for a little while and now I am home, little Ms. Nosey."

"I was on the phone with Rene today. She gave me an update on this Elizabeth Waters person. I was doing some research since I will be accompanying you on this trip out to Colorado. It was nice talking to her; I miss her and Junior."

Kingston listened as Tiana babbled on about the conversation she shared with Rene. When those two got together it was like rain and thunder.

Kingston loved his special time with Tiana. That girl's mouth ran a mile a minute. She had to know everybody's business; nothing got past her ears. If they did, Lord help us all.

Chapter 28

Janet

Janet pulled up, carrying the wine, sandwiches, and chocolate doughnuts. She prayed that Elizabeth was okay. Hearing her voice over the phone, it sounded like she had been crying and really need a friend. Janet rang the doorbell, waiting for Elizabeth to open up. Elizabeth opened the door, turning away, but Janet saw her eyes, red and puffy.

They walked to the kitchen to put down the snacks and wine. Janet was beating herself up for not helping Elizabeth and Leah. She was here now though, ready to be a shoulder to cry on.

"Hey kiddo, I am here for you to vent or curse as much as you need. Go ahead and lay it on me," Janet implored, opening her arms out to Elizabeth.

Elizabeth

Elizabeth walked over and gave Janet a hug as she broke down and cried again. Once Elizabeth was done, she looked at Janet's stained silk shirt due to her tears.

"I'm so sorry; I didn't mean to stain your shirt with my tears. You look nice, by the way," Elizabeth commented.

Janet was five-foot-three and one hundred and sixty pounds, with short black hair that she kept cut in a bob. She had green eyes and caramel skin.

"It's alright; don't worry about it. This is old and out of style. I should have worn my jeans with it instead of white slacks," Janet joked.

Elizabeth half-heartedly smiled, walking over to the kitchen counter to check out the goodies and wine Janet brought over to cheer her up.

"Oh, let me help with that while you talk; I will get this prepared for you," Janet insisted.

"I don't know how much more I am going to take. I can't deal with another broken heart. I fell in love with someone and now he doesn't want to be with me," Elizabeth confessed.

"I see, and what were his reasons for not wanting to being in a relationship with you?" Janet questioned.

"He is married with a family. We were all friends once upon a time, then his wife turned on me for no apparent reason. She works and goes to school. She is a complete bitch toward him. He served his country for years but she's still not happy. Their son came to my house and disrespected me. I don't deserve this."

Janet looked at her with concern. "Elizabeth, listen to me very carefully. I know that you are hurting, but you can't destroy another person's happiness just to feed your ego. It doesn't work that way. God isn't going to give you someone else's man. Find you a man that's not taken and wants you as much as you want him. There are plenty of them out there. I can introduce you to some of my friends." Janet smiled.

"I want the man I gave my heart to. Nobody can change my mind about him. We were meant for each other. Why can't nobody understand my feelings?"

"I understand your feelings. I have been in your shoes before. At least you know the man is married with a family. I didn't find out until after we slept together. By that time, I ruined that poor girl's marriage. I tried to apologize to her, but trust me she wasn't having none of that. She divorced him and took their unborn child with her. He doesn't even know where they are. It was like she disappeared. He went as far to hire an investigator spending all that money to find them, and still no luck."

Elizabeth listened as Janet continued.

"After what he did, I wouldn't be caught in the same store with him. He called me so many times that I had to change my number. There was no way I could continue to see him. If he cheated on her with me, it would be a matter of time before he would do it to me. Take my advice and leave this man alone. He will not leave his wife and family for you. You don't know anything about his wife's family background or friends. Pick and choose your battles carefully. You don't want to get caught up in a crossfire that you can't escape from. You got that sweet little girl to consider. I'm not saying that you should be alone; I am simply saying go after someone who is worth your time. And be careful; too many child molesters on the loose," Janet warned.

Elizabeth knew Janet was telling the truth but she wanted Sam and only Sam. If she couldn't have him, then she would make sure Rene wouldn't either.

Rene

I laid in bed, letting the tears flow. I didn't want Sam to think just because we had sex that everything was forgiven. I could hear him snoring softly in my ear. Trying not to disturb him, I slid out from his arm and grabbed my robe. I couldn't think with him in the room.

I went downstairs. Eating or drinking wasn't going to solve the problem. I thought about getting dressed and taking a ride on my motorcycle. That usually helped clear my mind. What I needed was to get out of the house and far away from Sam. I could feel a nervous breakdown coming on. With the possibility of Sam and Elizabeth sleeping together, I was becoming angrier by the second.

I felt like going back upstairs and beating the hell out of him. Changing my mind, I walked back upstairs to change clothes. It was time to take that ride. It had been a while since I had taken a ride on it to clear my head. Sam was still sound asleep, snoring as usual which didn't bother me at all. I was so confused. I knew it was too late to call my uncle Billy again to seek advice. I was going to drive over Elizabeth's house.

I wanted to end her miserable ass life. At the same time, I was trying not to let anger cloud my better judgement. It was close to midnight; this would be the perfection time. I grabbed my keys and opened the garage door, ready to hit the road.

Elizabeth

Elizabeth was taken by surprise that Janet had been involved with a married man. If he was still reaching out to her, then she should have kept going. His wife left him and he was free to date whomever he wanted. She didn't see any reason why Janet had to turn her back on him. She wondered if Janet was one of those types that believed "Once a cheater always a cheater".

Elizabeth would never cheat on Sam, not in a million years. Even though he had been cheating on Rene with her for several months and decided to end things between them. She was a fighter. To her, that was the number one problem with a lot of females: too afraid to fight for what they wanted.

She would not take another rejection.

"Janet, let me ask you this: were you in love with the guy?"

"Yes, but I was on a string. He wasn't worth it. As a woman, you have to be careful who you deal with. I had respect for myself. I will not share my man with anyone. I'm no side chick. If a man wants me, he has to be with me only."

Taking notes inside her head, Elizabeth agreed that she had respect for herself. Now it was war time. She would not go down without a fight. Pressing Janet for more information, this story might help her see things in a whole new perspective. They talked a little while longer, then it was time for Janet to leave.

Janet

As she was leaving, Janet thought about the time she had served in the military, and the man she was involved with. She was having serious feelings for the guy. She often thought about Sam. He was the one who had broken her heart into a million pieces. She thought about reaching out to him, but wondered if he thought about her as much as she thought about him.

Sam was seeing her, Rachel, and Rene but Rene was the one who he married. From what Sam told Janet, Rene had divorced him and took everything, including their child. That was some years ago. Maybe they could rekindle their romance and see if there was still a chance for them. Janet took out her phone to search his name on social media.

Rene

I was enjoying my ride. It was a peaceful night. I was thinking about my life with Sam and how I stayed with him after all these years. I believed in karma. Elizabeth would get what was coming to her sooner or later. It was only a matter of time. I thought back to the first time Sam cheated years ago. I had plenty of chances to cheat but I took my relationship with Sam very seriously. I just wanted to scream at the top of my lungs; even smash some things. I pulled over to the side of the road before I went too crazy.

Sam

I reached out for Rene but discovered she was not in bed with me. I quickly jumped out of bed to look for her. The entire house was quiet as a mouse. I went to the back door to see if she was in the garage and saw that her motorcycle was gone.

Closing the door, I picked up the phone to call her. It was dark and dangerous outside. Even though Rene could handle herself, I worried that someone might hurt her. She could have awakened me to let me know she was going out for a joy ride.

"Come on baby, answer your phone, where are you?"

She didn't answer. I was getting nervous. I redialed her number multiple times, wondering if she went to Elizabeth's house to confront her about our alleged affair.

Rene

I could see that Sam was calling me, but I wasn't in the mood to talk to him just yet. All I wanted was to be left alone for a while. He wasn't this worried when he was sleeping with different women behind my back. I was trying my best not to snap at him. I needed space and distance.

He kept calling. The only way to get a piece of mind was to talk to him for a few seconds.

"Yes! Sam what is it?" I asked.

"Thank God you are alright! I was worried about you. I reached out for you and realized that you were gone. You could have told me that you were going out for a ride on your bike. Where are you? It's late and you should be at home with me. I'm sorry I fell asleep. I wanted this night to be special. Come home so we can cuddle together. I don't like being without you. We can watch a movie together. I'm pretty sure there are some pretty good ones on tonight."

I was wondering what the hell was the matter with him? He was never this clingy before. Now I was sure that he was trying to cover up a secret.

"Sam, I wanted time and space alone. That's why I left. I wanted to get out of the house for a while to think and clear my head. I haven't had a moment to myself all day. I don't see what the big deal is. I am fine; I can take care of myself. Go back to bed. I will be on my way shortly."

"No, baby I am going to stay up and wait for you. I want to see you when you walk through the door. I love you with all my heart. I don't want nobody but you Rene; you are my world."

I hated when he would try to make things so complicated. He did that when he wanted to get out of the doghouse and back on my good side. I blamed myself for sleeping with him. I wished I didn't do that. Now he thought he had won the war and that all was forgiven.

"I will be there shortly; stop worrying about me."

I hung up before he had a chance to reply. This was not the Sam that I knew.

"Fuck you, Sam! What is it that you did that you are so desperate to keep me from finding out?" I snapped.

Elizabeth

Elizabeth went to check on Leah and she was still sound asleep. She quietly closed the door, not wanting to disturb her baby. She really needed to get out of the house, just for an hour or so. Leah was in a deep coma sleep. She would not wake up for another few hours. Elizabeth thought about taking a drive just to try and get Sam off her mind, which would be hard to do.

Going outside to take a look at the stars and the moon, she smiled to herself. It was rather warm out and she could use the distraction. Since everyone thought she was an evil monster, she would show them how evil she could be. Looking at her car, Elizabeth noticed that her tires were flat and slashed. Feeling her anger rising, she didn't know who could have done this to her, or why. In this neighborhood though, you couldn't be too careful.

Thank God, she always kept her Lexus in the garage. Elizabeth was always taught to keep a plan B. Leah was safe and sound. All the people in her neighborhood were still sleeping. Going back inside to retrieve her keys, she grabbed them, opening the door to the garage and feeling excited about her joy ride.

Making sure that she had tightly secured everything, with all the windows locked and leaving on the television for sound and turning on the lamp for extra light, Elizabeth went into the kitchen to get Leah's sippy cup just in case she woke up thirsty. Checking the batteries on the baby monitor, she would take the extra one with her. She kept baby monitors all over the house. She was going to protect her daughter at all costs.

Taking the sippy cup to her room, Elizabeth checked to make sure that Leah was dry as a bone before she left for a midnight cruise. Happy that she could get a little break from parenthood for a moment, she was going to take advantage of this. Getting inside her car to pull off into the night, Elizabeth was singing her favorite country song.

Letting the wind blow her long brown hair and feeling happy, she couldn't remember when the last time was that she was able to enjoy a nice midnight cruise where it was her, the darkness, and music blasting. Leaning her head back to feel the vibrant sensations of the music relaxing her, Elizabeth sang as loud as her lungs would allow to hit those high notes.

Rene

I was seething with rage. I knew I had a shopping and drink date with Shelby and I'd better get home to get some rest before we have our girls' day out. As I was about to get up and hop on my bike, I looked back and heard someone blasting country music and singing off key.

I got back on my bike and took off. Whoever was behind me was driving a little too fast. Speeding up, I could see the taillights that were flashing really bright. I cursed myself for not bringing my helmet.

Elizabeth

Elizabeth was enjoying her brief moment when she saw Rene on her motorcycle. She found herself speeding up get a better view. That's when she knew she couldn't pass up this chance. Pressing the accelerator pedal, she was going after Rene to send her to the gates of hell.

"I've got you now, bitch! I am going to get my Sam back, even if it means running your black ghetto ass over! It's dark; no one can identify me in a million years." Elizabeth laughed.

Elizabeth sped up, trying to catch Rene. The faster Rene drove her bike, the faster Elizabeth was on her tail.

Feeling out of control, Elizabeth crashed right into Rene, throwing her off her bike. Seeing Rene flying through the air caused Elizabeth no remorse at all. Pulling over, Elizabeth got out of the car and walked over to a badly injured Rene. She bent down, taking a look at her and laughing. She whispered into Rene's ear.

"I bet Sam doesn't want you now. Don't worry; I will take care of him. One person left to get rid of, and I will find a way to get rid of that brat of a son of yours too."

Getting up to leave, Elizabeth could hear Rene whisper, "Help me". Elizabeth ignored her as she walked back to her car. Leah would be her alibi.

Chapter 29

Sam

I was pacing back and forth. Rene said that she was on her way home. I continued to wait outside. I wanted my wife back.

I dialed her number again and she didn't answer. This wasn't fair. I loved her and wanted to come clean, but I knew that she would leave me for good. I prayed that she would hurry home soon.

Then I remembered the tracking device I had put on her phone a while back. I checked to see where her location was. I was going to find my wife and bring her home. Since she was on her bike, I would take the truck. That way, I could load it up. Rene might have run out of gas and got stranded.

Suddenly, I got the feeling that Rene was in danger and needed my help. I found the highway Rene was on and immediately recognized her bike laying on the side of the road.

My heart was racing a mile a minute. I was praying that someone had stolen her bike and fallen. I pulled over and jumped out, taking out my phone to turn on the flashlight to make sure whoever stole her bike was okay. I saw the bike's damages, which didn't matter to me. I got closer and saw Rene on the ground.

"Rene noooooooooo! Baby don't die on me!"

I quickly dialed 9-1-1 for help. I couldn't lose her; not like this. She couldn't pay for my mistakes. God couldn't take her away now. How was I going to explain this to Billy?

"911 operators; what's your emergency?"

"My wife has been in a serious accident. Please help me. Her name is Rene Smith. We are off the highway of Arkansas Valley. Send help now! I can't lose my wife."

"Okay sir, I am sending help. They are on their way now. Just stay on the phone with me until they arrive. Can you check for a pulse? Is she breathing?"

I checked for a pulse. It was there, but faint. I began to demonstrate CPR on her. I could tell she wasn't breathing.

"Sir, can you hear me? Please talk to me." I didn't want to talk anymore. I wanted to save Rene's life. I could hear the ambulance, fire truck, and police coming. Their colors flashed at a distance.

Finally, help arrived. I hung up. I couldn't let her go. The paramedics rushed over with their equipment, knocking me out of the way. The firemen were assisting the paramedics. I knew I'd better call Billy to tell him the news. I began crying as I saw how they were working extra hard to save her. One officer got out and tore me away from the scene.

"Hello, I am Officer Marsha. Can you tell me what happened tonight?"

I didn't want to talk to no officer. My mind was on Rene. Nothing else mattered right now. The tears were coming down my face. This was all my fault.

"I don't know what happened. My wife likes to cruise on her motorcycle at night. I was home and she told me she was on her way back. I started getting worried and I had a tracking device installed on her phone; that's how I was able to track her down."

I had my truck towed home. I wanted to be by Rene's side. I couldn't let her out of my sight.

The paramedics were loading Rene onto the stretcher. I raced over. "Will she be alright? Is my wife going to live? Please talk to me," I begged.

"Sir, she is very weak and we need to rush her to the hospital. She is still alive. You can ride in the back. Please stand aside, because we need to continue our work on her," the paramedic warned.

I climbed in the back with her, trembling and watching the love of my life fight for her life. I wanted to hold her hand but I agreed to stand aside, telling Rene that I loved her and not to give up.

My mind started racing as I wondered if it was a drunk driver or a person driving with road rage?

I wanted to be in the operating room with her. The nurse gave me medical forms to fill out, but I didn't want to be bothered with paperwork. I wanted to be by Rene's side, giving her my full attention and full support.

The nurse offered to help me fill out the medical forms. Once they were completed, I signed them. Looking up, I saw Officer Marsha coming in. I wasn't in the mood to talk to her. I just wanted to hear that Rene was okay.

"I lost my husband to a motorcycle accident a few years back, so I know how you are feeling. I will not ask how you are doing; I can see that for myself that you are in a state of shock. If she has family, they need to be notified immediately. If you want, I can make the calls for you, even though we are not supposed to."

I knew Marsha was trying to be helpful in any way she could, but the news had to come from me. Rene wasn't dead; just not responding. I kept looking at the emergency door where they had brought in her moments ago. Shaking my head, I called Billy, knowing that he would not be pleased with what he was about to hear.

Elizabeth

Going home, Elizabeth was smiling to herself. There was a reason she wanted to take that midnight drive; who would have thought Rene would be out this time of night, riding her motorcycle?

Hitting the button on her garage door to pull in, she turned off the motor. Feeling like a kid who got a good grade on her test, Elizabeth couldn't believe that Rene asked her for help. Hell no, Elizabeth wasn't going to call for help. She could have acted like the hero, which would have earned her some cool points with Sam. Maybe she didn't have to fake that pregnancy after all. All she had to do was wait until Sam came over to cry on her shoulders.

Once inside, she went to check on Leah. Sure enough, she was still sound asleep. Elizabeth checked the rest of the house and saw that everything was still the way she left it. When she reunited with Sam, it would be a happy ending.

Now that she had taken care of Rene, Elizabeth had to find a way to get rid of Junior. Taking out the bottle of wine and sandwiches Janet had prepared, Elizabeth felt that she deserved a treat. The real treat would come when she won back Sam.

Sam

Dr. Bentley came out, wiping the sweat off his face. I wasn't prepared to hear that my wife, the mother of my son, was dead.

"Hello Sam. I have good news and bad news; which do you want to hear first?" Dr. Bentley asked.

"Give it to me, Dr. I don't care. All I want to know is that my wife is still alive," I barked.

"Yes, she is very much still alive; that is the good news. The bad news is that we have her in the ICU. For a person who wasn't wearing a helmet, she was very lucky. She has lots of bruises, a broken collar bone, she has lost some blood, broken her left leg in two different places, and her right lung is punctured, which is why she was having a hard time breathing. It will take a while for all of her injuries to heal. Her rib cage was also bruised. I have no idea when she will wake up. Her eyes are swollen, but not shut. She got a shiner on both of them. I will be keeping a very close eye on her."

My prayers had been answered but I still needed to call Billy and tell him what happened. I tried to earlier, but froze up. Whoever did this to her would have hell to pay. I thanked Dr. Bentley for the latest update.

I called Shelby, and she answered. "Hello Shelby, it's Sam. I'm terribly sorry for waking you at this hour, but Rene was in an accident. She is in the hospital. I thought that I should let you know. Dr. Bentley is taking care of her."

It sounded like Shelby shot up in bed.

"Dr. Bentley is a very good doctor; what happened?" Shelby asked with concern.

"Shelby, it's a long story and I need to call Billy and tell him. We can talk in the morning. Go back to sleep."

Billy and Kingston were going to beat the hell out of me. I was responsible for Rene being in the hospital. I was still praying that she would not go into the light, even though Dr. Bentley assured me about her injuries.

Shelby

Hanging up, Shelby got out of her bed. She thought to call Kingston. She'd better get dressed because he would want her to go up the to the hospital and take care of his family. Why did she get the feeling the accident had Elizabeth's name written all over it? Quickly calling Kingston, she knew he was not going to be happy about this. She should have told Rene and Sam what Elizabeth was up to.

"Hello?" Kingston answered.

"Hello Kingston; I'm so sorry to be calling you so late but I need to tell you that Rene is in the hospital. She has been in a terrible accident. Sam called me. Dr. Bentley is an excellent doctor, but I am on my way there now," Shelby explained.

Kingston

Kingston couldn't believe it. He knew once he called and told Billy what happened, he would blow a gasket. Kingston quickly got out of bed to get dressed. He would wake Tiana to inform her, praying that Rene survived this accident.

"Thank you for calling and yes, please go to the hospital and be our eyes and ears until we get there. I appreciate you calling me."

He went down the hall to wake Tiana. He would explain everything on the way when they went to go and pick up Billy.

Dialing Billy's number to deliver the bad news, he knew his brother would not be able to control himself when he heard what he was about to tell him.

"Hello? This better be important," Billy answered.

"It's Kingston. Shelby just called me to tell me that Rene is in the hospital. She is on her way up there. You be packed and ready to go by the time I get there. I don't know all of the details of how this happened, but she will be our eyes and ears until we touch ground."

Billy was fully awake now. "What the hell do you mean, Shelby will be our eyes and ears? I want the full damn story! Kingston, I can't lose my little girl. And why didn't that son of a bitch Sam call us the minute she was hurt?" Billy yelled.

"I don't know. Shelby is a doctor and works there. I don't know what happened. I will touch base with her when I can. I need you to stay calm right now. Rene needs all of us, okay? I am on my way; just be ready."

Shelby

Shelby knew that Elizabeth was responsible for this accident. She would be held accountable for her actions. Shelby would tell Rene's family about Elizabeth and her connection with her. She at least owed Rene that much. She knew Elizabeth was in love with Sam, but she never thought that she would stoop this far as to try to kill his wife.

The last time Shelby felt this mad was when she was raped by her college professor and the charges were dismissed by the school board. Saying a silent prayer, she hoped Rene would make a full recovery. Before she went to the hospital, Shelby decided to make a stop at Elizabeth's house.

Billy

Billy couldn't believe Rene was hurt. He looked at her picture that he kept by his nightstand. He loved her so much. Trying not to let the tears come out, he knew he had to stay strong for her and Junior. What really set him off was that Sam wouldn't pick up the damn phone. Calling Sam's phone yet again, he had a book of words for him. When he saw him, he would knock the living hell out of him. Continuing to look at Rene's picture, Billy did the one thing he hadn't done in a long time. He picked up Rene's picture and prayed.

Chapter 30

Elizabeth

Elizabeth was wondering why Sam hadn't called or texted her yet. She would be patient. After all, Rene was just in a motorcycle accident. She was pretty sure somebody had reported it by now, or maybe Rene died at the scene? It was late at night. Only truck drivers were out at this time.

She would wait until Sam came crying in her arms. Checking her phone to make sure it was fully charged, Elizabeth's eyes grew heavy with sleep. She'd been up reading about how people died from motorcycle accidents. She wished that she would have thought of the idea months ago; then she would have been married to Sam and living in his beautiful home already.

Shelby

Shelby couldn't get dressed fast enough. She was looking forward to seeing Kingston; too bad it wasn't a happy occasion. She knew Elizabeth had gone way too far this time. She had completely snapped. Getting her keys and purse to make the trip to Elizabeth's house, Shelby had to remember that she was about to go heads up with the devil's daughter, one on one.

Billy

Billy didn't have time. He knew Kingston would be arriving at any moment. Setting down Rene's picture, he placed another call to Sam before making the trip to

Colorado. Billy could feel his blood pressure boiling like hot lava. Sam finally answered, sounding surprised that Billy called him.

"Hi Billy, I was about to call you after I was done talking to the doctor who is taking care of Rene," Sam explained.

"If my baby girl dies, you will die with her. I don't know what the hell is going on between you and that fat bitch Elizabeth, but I will find out when I get there. I know you and her are responsible for putting Rene in the hospital. When I get there, you better tell me every damn thing. If I find out that you lied to me about the color of your underwear, I will fucking kill you. Now will be your only time to come clean. I suggest that you take me seriously. That is my family, my blood laying in that hospital bed when it should have been you. I hate the ground that you walk on. I want the full damn story," Billy warned.

Billy disconnected the call before Sam had a chance to reply. He didn't want to hear any more of his lies. All he wanted was for Rene to divorce Sam and take Junior with her. If she was that afraid to leave him or if he had threatened her in any kind of way, Billy would provide all the protection that she needed.

Shelby

Shelby pulled over and parked on the side of the street. She was ready to take Elizabeth one on one. There was no turning back, but her time was very limited. She needed to get to the hospital to make sure Rene was getting the best treatment and care until Kingston arrived.

Getting out her car, she looked at Elizabeth's vehicle and saw that her tires had been slashed. Shelby wondered who would do such a thing. Then she remembered that Elizabeth lived in the hood, where anything goes. Shelby could see the garage light was on. She hoped that no one broke in and tried to rob her sister. Elizabeth didn't have anything that was worth stealing or pawning.

Then Shelby noticed something was off. She looked at Elizabeth's Lexus, sitting in the open garage. Where did she get the money to pay for that? The more Shelby was looking at the car, the more she felt there was something about that car that seemed off. Shelby wasn't a mechanic though. She would have to come back to snoop and take pictures. Maybe she could prove that Elizabeth was the one who hurt Rene.

Walking up the steps to the front door, Shelby didn't care if Elizabeth was awake or not. She would warn her that she wasn't getting away with this.

Shelby knocked on Elizabeth's door, waiting for her to come answer it. She wasn't leaving until she opened the door.

Elizabeth

When Elizabeth realized that someone was knocking, she smiled. She knew Sam would come back to her. Happy that at least one of her plans worked, she got up. Elizabeth was ready to get into character as the supportive new lady in his life. Taking her time walking to the door, she cleared her throat before she greeted him.

Opening the door to find Shelby standing there, Elizabeth frowned. This was not the time to come by for a chat. It was supposed to be Sam standing there, not her sister. Shelby walked right in, not waiting for Elizabeth to invite her.

"You are one deranged, sick ass bitch! I know that you have something to do with Rene being in the hospital," Shelby accused.

Elizabeth wondered how in the hell Shelby knew about Rene's accident? Was she following her? Did she see what happened? Elizabeth was feeling nervous. If Shelby saw her, that meant she would go straight to the police and report her.

"I have no clue to what you are talking about, and for the record, I have Leah: when would I have the time to hurt Rene? I don't appreciate that the fact that you came over to accuse me of a crime that I haven't committed. I think you better apologize to me," Elizabeth barked.

"I'm not apologizing for shit! You're right; I don't know how or when you had the time, but from what I saw outside, your car is on a flat with slash tires, but the Lexus that is parked in your garage, where did you get the money to buy it? We both know you haven't work since they fired you. To keep the light on in your garage is very strange. I don't put shit past you.

Ever since you met Sam and Rene, you have been obsessed with him. Even to go as far as to try and have me help you fake a pregnancy test. You are capable of a lot of things. Never in a million years would I have thought that you would go kill that man's wife, or at least try to?" Shelby snarled.

"Once again, I have no idea what the hell is going on. And don't worry about how I support myself and my daughter; that is none of your business," Elizabeth snapped. "Who told you about Rene anyway? Was it on the news and you just had to rush over to tell me about it? Honestly, I really don't give a damn about the bitch's accident. We stopped being friends a long time ago. My love for Sam is different. Last time I checked, you didn't want to help me. You left me no choice but to expose you and your family. If anyone is capable of murder, it's you! Didn't you kill a patient who was your college professor and also your rapist?"

Shelby marched right up to Elizabeth's face like she was about to knock her on her ass.

"Mark my words: you will get what's coming to you. This time, you have crossed the line. When Rene makes a full recovery, she will come back with a vengeance. You will have no one to blame but yourself. You want to expose me and my powerful family? Go ahead. I am on my way to the hospital and I'm going to expose you to Sam and Rene's family about your fake pregnancy." Shelby smirked.

"Wait! You can't be serious; if you do, then that I will lose Sam forever. Let me refrain from exposing you. I will keep your secrets only if you help me get Sam back. That's all I want. I have no idea who would want to hurt Rene that badly to put her in the hospital, but it wasn't me."

Kingston

Kingston was set and ready to go. Tiana and Genesis were still asleep.

He woke Tiana up and told her what happened. She sprang into action immediately, packing her and Genesis' things.

Tiana

Putting Genesis in his car seat, Tiana had already emailed her job and school and told them she had to leave on a family emergency.

Getting in the car, she closed her eyes, praying that God would spare Rene's life. She just couldn't take losing another dear family member. She already lost LillyMae and Chase. She came really close to losing Genesis. She didn't want to lose Rene. Sam, she cared less about. She knew there was something sneaky about him from the first time they met.

Tiana put on her tough brave face. She couldn't show any emotion right now. She saw Kingston trying to steal a couple of looks at her. She knew what he was thinking.

"You do know that Rene is going to be alright. I know that you have a million questions to ask, but I don't have the answers to them. I do know Shelby will be our eyes and ears until we touch bases. I have talked to Billy. He will be ready. He should be packed and already. Our plane leaves in four hours. I know that you were doing some research on Elizabeth - I was wondering if you could shed some light and tell me what you found out?" Kingston entreated.

Tiana didn't want to talk about it with him. That was a conversation between her and Rene. They were forming their own plan to get even with Elizabeth. She also knew that Kingston would keep hassling her until she gave him some type of answer. Opening her eyes to talk, she decided to withhold certain things from him, like the address she found online.

That was one of the reasons Tiana enjoyed studying criminal justice. She could learn about anyone's life history. She was naturally nosey, just like LillyMae had always told her from the time she was born.

"I know that her last name is Waters and she bounced around from foster home to from foster home. She has one daughter who is three years old. She has served time in prison; only five years. She was born in Texas. I couldn't get a hold of her birth records yet, but I will. She isn't that much older than Rene."

Kingston

Kingston nodded at Tiana's information. He could easily get a hold of Elizabeth's birth records. That wasn't a problem at all. Tiana was a lot smarter than most people gave her credit for; he had to hand it to her. They both stayed silent until they reached Billy's house. Kingston turned on the radio so the music could cut some of the tension that lingered in the air.

Billy

Seeing Kingston drive up, Billy didn't waste any time picking up his bags. He placed them in the car, rushing back to lock up his house. He wasn't worried about anyone breaking in. He always kept it booby trapped with hidden cameras. Denzel Washington wasn't the only one who knew about James Bond's secrets. Billy's mind was on keeping Rene alive.

Once he got inside the car, they all exchanged hellos. He looked to see Genesis still sleeping. Tiana was a great mother. So was Rene. Just thinking about Junior being a motherless child, Billy knew how that felt. It was a pain that never went away.

"I called that bastard Sam and told him what I thought about his ass," Billy announced. "I just couldn't wait any longer. I also set up a fake profile on Facebook earlier. I had to get some inside scoop on Elizabeth, the dummy. I haven't brought out the big guns yet; I just need to get close enough for her to tell me if there is more to her friendship with Sam."

Kingston and Tiana exchanged glances. Billy knew it was because they didn't think he knew anything about computers, let alone social media. Tiana burst out laughing and Kingston cracked a smile. At least they had some type of information.

They made it in the nick of time to the Memorial Airport. Taking their bags out, Billy and Kingston offered to get Tiana's bags while she attended to Genesis.

Tiana

Tiana was standing in line waiting to get checked in. She was ready to get this show on the road. She was terrified of airplanes. She didn't want it to crash, not when Rene needed her the most. Kingston patted her on the shoulder. Tiana smirked as she looked up at him to let him know she was fine.

The attendant announced their flight. It was time to take off. Giving the attendant their tickets as they were boarding, Tiana wanted a drink to calm her nerves. She wondered when Rene flew, did she drink or take a sedative before the plane took off?

Kingston

Kingston and Billy sat across from Tiana and Genesis. They could both sense that Tiana wasn't ready to stomach another death. Deep down, Kingston couldn't either. They had to work as a team and stick together.

Kingston turned to his brother. "Hey, I need to know you didn't blow a gasket on Sam after I got off the phone with you."

"Naw, I wanted to, but I figured Rene wouldn't want that right now. I just can't seem to figure out this damn connection between Sam and Elizabeth," Billy answered.

"Neither can I. It's more to this than what he is telling us. Rene is smart. She was born in the dark, but not last night. There is no way that woman could be this infatuated by him if he wasn't sleeping with her. If not, then it's something," Kingston said.

"I only wish that I would have forced her to file for that damn divorce."

Kingston didn't say anything, buckling his seat belt before they took off. He forgot to check his phone to see if Shelby had gotten back to him. He would when he got a chance. He heard the stewardess make her announcement. It was about to go down.

Chapter 31

Sam

I was a nervous wreck. I didn't know which way to turn. I was retired from the military, but still connected to my military friends. I could call them if I needed to cash in on some serious favors. I still hadn't called Junior. This had to be the longest day of my entire life.

I started reminiscing about my parents. They were like night and day. My father used to beat the hell out of me, and my mother Avery would look the other way. One night, I was in my room minding his own business, listening to music and playing with my dog. My dad came home angry because I left a dirty plate in the sink. He immediate began screaming at me.

I turned down the music and came out of my room. I could see my father with a shotgun, sitting at the kitchen table. I was too afraid to go near him. I was easing my way to the front door and my dad caught me, slapping me hard in the back of the head. I fell down and my dad continued by kicking me in the ribs. I turned over to see the gun pointing between my eyes. At that very moment, something inside of me snapped. I found the strength to fight him man to man.

Dad couldn't believe I would fight him. We struggled, and I got the upper hand. I wasn't about to give up. I wrestled the gun out of his hand and turned it on my father. I saw fear in his eyes for once.

"Okay son; I will give you anything that you want; just don't kill me," Dad pleaded.

"There is nothing that you can give me," I replied.

That's when I pulled the trigger, shooting my dad in the head and killing him instantly. I got myself cleaned up, then went to my room and packed my clothes, taking the money I was saving after telling my parents that I had been accepted into the United States Army.

We lived in a wooded area, so neighbors were a distance away. I buried his body in the backyard along with his shotgun after cleaning the gun, tile floors, and walls of all evidence. I made sure to smooth the area where I buried him over so that what I had done wouldn't be detected any time soon. Once everything was set to my liking, I wrote my mother Avery a heartfelt letter and grabbed my duffle bag, closing the door behind me. I never went back there again.

Elizabeth

Elizabeth tried her best to regain control of the situation, but Shelby wouldn't see things her way, no matter what she said or did. She was just wasting time and breath.

Shelby had rushed to her car to go rat her out to Sam. Elizabeth couldn't allow that, but she thought about it: what proof did Shelby have that she was involved? Sam wouldn't believe her.

Walking to the back door to make sure there were no damage to her vehicle, Elizabeth took a quick glance. The garage was chilly. She didn't have on her shoes. A light bulb went off in her head; she knew how she could stop Shelby from spoiling her plan.

Closing the door, she put on her shoes and walked out the front door. Whoever slashed her tires had just saved her life. She would blame Shelby for the damage.

"Thank you, sis, you just made my day." Elizabeth smiled to herself.

Going back inside, Elizabeth called the police to report that her car was damaged and vandalized, and to say she needed an officer to come to her home at once. It didn't take very long for them to arrive. Elizabeth opened the door to meet them outside. She went outside to see them looking at her car.

"Hi, I'm Officer Marsha and this is my partner, Robert."

The male officer tipped his hat, taking out his pad and pen to get ready to take notes.

"It's nice to meet you both," Elizabeth greeted.

"Tell me what happened?" Marsha stated.

"Dr. Shelby Henderson came over and we got into a heated argument. I was here with my three-year-old daughter who is asleep inside. Shelby blamed me for her life not being as glamourous as she hoped for. I was having a mother daughter day, then she just snapped on me. I was asleep, then she started yelling at me about some motorcycle accident. I had no idea who was she talking about. I didn't hear it on the news.

I was friends with a lady named Rene Smith. She owns a motorcycle and loves to ride it late at night off the Arkansas Valley. I haven't seen or spoken to her. When I told Shelby that she was crazy, she came out here and damaged my tires. I have my daughter to protect, and if damaging my car is going to make her feel better than fine," Elizabeth stated.

Marsha and Robert exchanged glances. Elizabeth wasn't sure what that meant. Her story sounded good to her ears. Officer Robert was writing everything that Elizabeth had described.

"Do you want to press charges against her?" Officer Robert asked.

"Yes! I want her arrested. She will not get away with this kind of destructive behavior. I will not tolerate it. She works at the Denver Community Hospital. She is on her way there now. She just left after I called you guys for help."

"Alright, we will go there and see if we can find her. Robert, run her name and see if there is an address that we can use, or anything else that might be helpful," Officer Marsha ordered.

Robert closed the pad and did as he was told, taking a look at Elizabeth. Elizabeth wondered what that was about.

"Is there anything else I need to know before I go?" Officer Marsha asked.

Elizabeth debated if she should tell them that Shelby killed her professor who raped her when she was in medical school, but she decided to save that for when the right time came. Right now, this was a calling card to Shelby.

"No, that is all. I will have a friend of mines who fixes cars come and check change my tires. It won't take him very long. Besides, my car is in desperate need of some repairs to make sure that it is safe for me to drive." Elizabeth smiled.

"Okay, make sure you get it taken care of. We will find Shelby and bring her in, but you will need to come down to the precinct to file the necessary paperwork since you are pressing charges," Officer Marsha advised.

Shelby

Shelby arrived at the hospital, parking in her assigned parking space. Collecting her things getting out of her car and locking it up, she thought that she needed to talk to Sam privately after she got an update on Rene's condition. Rushing inside, she saw Dr. Bentley. She stopped him before he went to continue his rounds.

"Dr. Bentley, I just heard that Rene Smith is here. She was my patient years ago when I delivered her son. Please tell me that she will make it?" Shelby asked with concern.

"Dr. Henderson, you know that I am an excellent doctor and do not like to discuss my patient's wellbeing, but I will say this: yes, she will live, but she'll be out of commission for a while. I have spoken to her husband. He is fully aware of her condition."

"Thank you. I will go see how he is doing." Shelby smiled as she walked to find Sam.

Quickly scanning the room in search of Sam, she saw him sitting in the waiting area staring into space. Shelby felt so sorry for the guy. He was a nice guy; all he wanted to do was make his marriage work, love his wife, and be happy. Elizabeth was doing everything that she could to destroy it. Shelby thanked God that Rene would live to tell everyone that Elizabeth was the one who attempted to kill her.

"Hey. I came as soon as I could." Shelby took a seat next to Sam.

"Thank you for coming, which you didn't have to. I should have never fallen asleep. I should have gone after her and brought her back home, but she told me that she was on her way. I told her that I would wait for her.

Thank God that I have tracking. That's how I found her," Sam confessed.

"It's alright; no one blames you. But there is something that you need to know about Elizabeth. I was going to wait to tell Rene when we were going to have a girl's day out. I can see her family isn't here yet, so I am going to tell you that you need to be extra careful around Elizabeth. She is planning a fake pregnancy to try to win you back, hoping that Rene will divorce you. She asked me to help her. I told her no."

Sam turned in his seat to look at Shelby.

"How do you know Elizabeth? And why didn't you say anything to us before? We could have stopped her!"

"Elizabeth and I are sisters. There is more to the story than what is being told. Plus, I didn't know if you and Rene would be upset with me. I really like Kingston and I just didn't want to make things hard for you guys. I thought we all could have stopped her. My history with her is completely different from yours."

Sam

I was at a loss for words. I wondered if Elizabeth hurt Rene tonight? If she was this vindictive to make up such lies, then just how far would she go to try to get me to come back to her?

"I have to ask you this even though it's not important, but were you going to help her frame me?" I studied Shelby's face as she spoke.

She shook her head. "No, I wasn't. Like I said, it's a long story between me and Elizabeth. Right now we need to focus on Rene. She is what matters. Did you call Junior yet? I don't see him around."

I couldn't believe that Elizabeth was a psycho. I didn't have anyone to blame but myself. I started it when I allowed her to give me oral sex.

Tiana

Tiana, Kingston, and Billy couldn't wait for the plane to land. It seemed like they had been flying in the air forever. They couldn't believe that Rene was in the hospital fighting for her life, and it was all Sam and Elizabeth's fault.

Tiana couldn't make up her mind about who she should knock out first. Even though she wanted to hit Sam first, she would let Kingston and Billy handle him.

Billy

Billy was looking out the window, trying not to explode. He wanted to get to Rene faster than a speeding bullet. Repeatedly checking his watch, the more he checked the time, the slower it went. He prayed that Rene hadn't given up and left him alone forever. Billy tried to change the negative thoughts from his mind.

Kingston

Kingston could feel his pressure rising. He needed to check his phone as soon as they landed to see if Shelby had made it to the hospital to keep an eye on Rene. He felt so helpless; he couldn't imagine how Billy was feeling. He knew for sure that he was trying to keep the murderous side hidden until he touched ground. Kingston knew if Tiana was hurt and laying in the hospital or had died, he would beat the hell out of the person. No question about it.

"Hey bro, don't worry. We will take care of this. I'm sure that Rene is going to make a full recovery. She is strong and tough, just like you. She will never leave you. She got a son to raise and a lot of life to live," Kingston reassured Billy.

"Thanks bro; right now, I need this fucking plane to land. I need to get to her asap. I will tell you this: when I see Sam's punk ass, I will be knocking him the fuck out."

The pilot announced that they would be landing at the Denver International Airport momentarily.

Chapter 32

Janet

Janet was thinking about Sam after leaving Elizabeth's house. It was like their conversation sparked an avalanche of memories. Although she told Elizabeth to leave her man alone, Janet couldn't believe she let Sam get away all those years ago. She should have fought for him instead of giving up so easily. She had missed him so much. Sam wanted to keep her as a side chick or sex buddy, or even as friends. Janet thought of how selfish he was; a disgrace to her and her family.

When Rene came between them by sending her two uncles after Sam, they almost killed him. Rene wanted a divorce. Janet didn't apologize because she was sorry about sleeping with Sam. She went to apologize because she felt sorry for Sam marrying Rene and getting her pregnant.

Janet also hated Sam for making her get an abortion because he didn't want two different baby mamas. He was in love with Rene because he said she kept him grounded. She was there for him when he felt like giving up and wanted to end his life. There was no way that he could give her up now that she was having his baby.

Janet wanted to claw his eyes out when she heard him say that. She was good enough to fuck on whenever he wanted to but wasn't good enough for him to marry and have a family with. She wished that she would have kept the baby, but she didn't want a child out of wedlock and was in the military herself. Who would have been there to help raise the baby while she served her country?

Now Elizabeth had fallen in love with a married man who loved his wife. Janet prayed that Elizabeth took her advice seriously. Janet did have sex with Sam one last time and Rene had followed them to a cheap motel and caught them red handed. Janet was close to getting her head blown off. That was the final straw for her, despite the fact that Sam later told her that Rene had run off with his son. Sam wasn't worth losing her life over.

Billy

Billy couldn't wait to get off the plane. He had some serious ass whipping to do. He had warned Sam about fucking with him when it came to his family and now, he was done talking. It was time for some action.

Tiana

Tiana was grateful for the trip, but this wasn't the trip she had in mind. At least Genesis would get to spend more time with Junior and Tiana would meet Shelby in person and not through video chat.

Kingston

Kingston was looking forward to hearing the lies that Sam was about to tell him. The way Billy was talking, Kingston knew he would shoot to kill and not think twice about it. They helped Tiana and Genesis get out of their seat so they could collect their bags and go straight to the hospital.

Shelby

Sam looked at Shelby. "No, I haven't called Junior yet. I have to get my thoughts together before I make the call. Maybe he can spend another night at Jose's house. I feel so drained and confused."

Shelby understood where Sam was coming from. She had thought that she had a connection with her late husband, Larry, until he got hooked on drugs and alcohol. Then he started to change into a different person that she didn't recognize or even know. He was an evil monster. Every day it got worse until the abuse was started to take its toll on her.

Each time he would apologize, and she would fall for it. The final straw was when he got so plastered that he crashed into a tree, nearly killing them. Thank God, she had survived; wearing her seatbelt was what had saved her life. Larry died instantly. It was the best day of her life, but it was also the worst day. She was free from him, but she loved him. Not the monster side of him, but lovable side that she had first met.

Kingston

Kingston checked his phone. No word from Shelby. He hoped it wasn't bad as he thought. Not waiting any longer, he decided to call her to see what she found out about Rene's condition. Dialing Shelby's phone number, he hoped to hear some kind of good news.

"Hello," Shelby said in a pleasant voice.

"Hi, I'm letting you know that we are here. Waiting for a cab to come, then we will be headed that way. I should have made arrangements to rent a car. How is Rene?" Kingston asked.

"I'm glad that everyone is here. I spoke to Dr. Bentley and he wouldn't discuss Rene with me but he is one million percent sure that she will live and make a full recovery. I'm talking to Sam. He can give you a better update than I can. Poor fella; he is really hurting. He hasn't even called Junior to tell him. He was the one who had found her by using a GPS tracking device."

Kingston wasn't impressed. Sam hadn't hurt yet.

"Okay, I will let the others know." Kingston said, hanging up.

Shelby

Shelby felt goosebumps after she hung up with Kingston.

"Sam, Rene's family came to town. They will be here at any moment. I just hope that they won't blame you for what happen to Rene. It's not your fault; I feel that Elizabeth is somehow involved in this. I went by her place and her tires were slashed and on a flat, then I see that she's got a Lexus parked inside her garage. It's something about that damn car that is really bugging me," Shelby explained.

"Why would she want to hurt Rene?" Sam asked. "When would she find the time to run her down when she has Leah 24/7? That would nearly be impossible, unless she had someone to come over and watch her while she followed Rene late at night. That sounds absurd; don't you think?"

"Sam, if she is willing to fake a pregnancy test, there is no telling what other trick she might pull next. Did you know that Elizabeth served time in prison for money laundering? That's just one of many charges. She only served five years out of twenty because she took a plea deal and ratted out the other people that were involved."

Sam

I looked at Shelby, stunned. Elizabeth was definitely cut from a different cloth. It would take more than a protective order to keep her away from me.

Kingston

Kingston turned to Billy. "Hey bro, I just got off the phone with Shelby. Rene is very much alive and will make a full recovery. Dr. Bentley is taking good care of her. That is all the information that I got about Rene. Shelby also pointed out that Sam is hurting. I call bullshit on that one."

"The cab just pulled up. Let's go. I can't wait to face off with that son of a bitch." Billy scoffed.

They loaded their bags into the cab and were ready to go to war.

Chapter 33

Elizabeth

Elizabeth checked on Leah, happy that she was still asleep. Then she wondered if there were any damages to her Lexus that she didn't see. She didn't want blood or evidence about the hit-and-run accident leading back to her. Grabbing her jacket and shoes, she decided to inspect it more thoroughly.

Walking briskly to the kitchen door, she cursed herself for leaving the garage light on. She thought that she had turned it off. Going to see if there was evidence, Elizabeth looked carefully. She couldn't afford to make any mistakes. Checking from the front to back, Elizabeth ran her hands along the sides of the car.

"Oh fuck! My damn headlight is busted. Fuck me. Oh no! There is blood. Everything is damn near destroyed. This can send me up the river. I have to get rid of this car. Maybe if I remove this license plate, that will keep me in the clear," Elizabeth said in a panic.

"Think Elizabeth, think! I have to get rid of this fucking car without it being traced back to me. But how?"

Going back inside and feeling cold chills running through her body, Elizabeth knew this wasn't part of the plan. She didn't know who to call. She couldn't drive the car; then people would notice it and might report her to the police. Going back into the garage to look inside, Elizabeth noticed that Leah's baby monitor was gone. Looking at the GPS computer on the dashboard, it led her to the accident where she had run over Rene. She didn't know how to uninstall it.

Feeling frightened, Elizabeth reasoned that there was no way she was going down for murder. She could always take Leah and go away, never to return. Nobody could point the finger at her if she wasn't home. She could call Janet and see if she wanted to take a road trip.

But where would we go? Elizabeth thought.

She could feel the walls starting to cave in on her. Elizabeth couldn't breathe; she had to get out of there. Going back inside and closing the door, she cursed herself for not covering her damn tracks last night.

The only person who could help her was Janet. Dialing's Janet number and waking her up was the best chance she had. There was no time to waste. She would leave a window up; that's how someone got inside her home.

"Hello Janet, I was wondering, do you want to take a road trip? I need a break from Colorado and so does Leah."

"Elizabeth, it's too early to be thinking about a road trip right now. Besides, I don't have any money. Where would we go anyway? Don't get me wrong; it does sounds nice to get away. The closest place for us to go to would be Las Vegas. I have a few friends out there that have been wanting me to come out that way."

"That's perfect. Let's go. We can be ready in an hour. I need a ride to the police station, girl. Shelby came to my house and slashed my tires and flattened them. I already made a report of it. I want to press charges against her. Please, let's go. I have money on my bank card. We can use that for gas, and I have my food stamps. We can buy as much as we need for the trip."

"I'm sorry Elizabeth, but the answer is no," Janet said, hanging up.

Elizabeth stared at her phone, stunned. How could Janet be so selfish? She offered to pay for everything! All Janet had to do was point her to her stupid friends in Vegas, and Elizabeth and Leah would be all set. Elizabeth was back to talking to herself again. "I got to get out of here now, but who can help me change two flat tires on a short notice? I can't believe this! Where is a crack head in this neighborhood when you need one?" she mumbled.

Going outside, she looked at her neighbor. Once again, God had answered her prayers.

"Hey, Rodney. Do you want to make twenty bucks? I need two tires changed on my car; can you help a sister out?" Elizabeth asked.

"Be right there. I have spare tires that will fit your car. I'll will bring them over, and tools." Rodney shot her a suggestive look after he said that, like he was expecting more than twenty dollars for giving her the two tires. Elizabeth played along, letting him think what he wanted. By the time he figured it out, she would be long gone.

Elizabeth smiled. She felt herself relax a bit. Now she could get Leah up and dressed to withdraw as much cash as she could and buy as much food as she would need for the road trip. Elizabeth went back inside to start breakfast and pack her bags.

Billy

Billy was getting more anxious every second riding in the taxi cab. He wished he would drive faster.

Finally arriving at the hospital, the driver dropped them off at the main entrance. Billy and Kingston told Tiana to go ahead. They would catch up to her.

Tiana

Tiana couldn't wait to slap the taste out of Sam's mouth, then let her uncles deal with him. Going to the front desk, Tiana asked for Rene Smith's room. The nurse at the front desk gave Tiana information and directions. Tiana waited for her uncles before she continued. Billy and Kingston came in. Following Tiana, they saw Sam talking to Shelby.

Billy dropped his bags and rushed over to Sam, driving right into him with a left blow. Kingston and Tiana stood by, letting Billy have his way with Sam.

The nurses called for security.

Shelby yelled at both of them to stop before they got thrown out. She tried her best to break them up. Officer's Marsha and Robert arrived out of nowhere and rushed over to assist Shelby. Security also came to help calm Billy down.

Kingston

Shelby went over to hug Kingston. He returned her embrace.

"I'm glad you're here it's really nice to see you again." Shelby said while smiling.

Kingston lifted his lips back at her. Usually, he would flash his famous smile, but it would have to wait until they were alone. Deep down he felt the same way about Shelby that she felt about him. Tiana cleared her throat to remind them that it was not the time to play Romeo & Juliet. They turned their attention to Billy, Sam, and the officers.

Sam was rubbing the side of his jaw after the officers pulled him and Billy apart.

"You motherfucker!" Billy ranted. "Don't you think for one second that I'm done, 'cause I'm not. We will finish this conversation. That's my fucking baby in there fighting her damn life and it's all your fault. If you would have stayed away from Elizabeth, she wouldn't be in there now, motherfucker."

Officers Marsha and Robert were trying their best to hold Billy back. They had already explained that they didn't want to arrest him since they gathered he was upset over the family matter, but they would if they had to. "Alright pal; take it easy. You need to calm down. I understand that you are upset, but maybe you can answer some questions for us. If you don't calm down, we will arrest you," Officer Robert reminded Billy again.

Kingston walked over to stand by officer Robert and crossed his arms.

"Let my brother go right now," Kingston said in his deep Barry White voice.

Billy

The two officers looked at Kingston. Billy knew once Kingston's voice went deep, he meant business. Billy stopped resisting so they would let him go and he straightened out his clothes, not taking his eyes off Sam.

Kingston took charge. "Billy, go take Tiana with you to see Rene. Do not look back."

Billy and Tiana obeyed.

Kingston

Kingston focused on Sam. "Sam, I am not in the mood for games. My family's life is at stake, which means you need to bring your black ass over here and sing like Patty Labelle; I will say it one time."

Officers Marsha and Robert nodded their approval and took out their pads and pens, getting ready to take notes.

Before either officer could ask questions, Kingston decided he was the new law enforcer. He didn't give a damn about the pigs standing in front of him.

"Sam stall me out with the bullshit, because you have lied to me more than once. If you love Rene, you will speak up. Yes or no: did you have sex with Elizabeth?" Kingston questioned.

Sam swallowed, then spoke. He looked at the cops. "Yes! I have been fucking on her for months. Now she is trying to get Shelby to help her pull a fake pregnancy just so that Rene will divorce me," Sam admitted.

Kingston wanted to break every bone in Sam's body when he heard that, but he would give Billy the pleasure of doing that.

"Continue with the story. Do not stop talking until I say so," Kingston barked.

Officer Marsha opened her mouth to interrupt, but Sam started talking, so she shut it.

"It started out that we were all friends, then Rene started working, going back to school, and bitching at me for not working. It was so much going on between us. Then Elizabeth moved next door and we started talking as friends. She was friends with Rene first. I guess I got in the way of that when Rene left to go to school. I stepped outside for a smoke and Elizabeth invited me over for breakfast. She performed oral sex on me."

Kingston listened as Sam continued, becoming more enraged as he spoke.

Sam had gone and cheated on Rene again. She needed to really leave him for good this time.

What wifey won't do, my sidepiece will, Kingston thought to himself.

"What is Elizabeth's address? I want to get her side of the story," Kingston insisted.

The Officers tried to stop it, but Sam spoke before they could.

"927 East Olive Street," Sam testified.

"You can't go there," Officer Marsha stated.

Kingston played it cool. "I know I can't, Officers," he said, finally addressing them. "I was just trying to help you with your investigation, since you are apparently terrible at your jobs."

Officer Robert looked appalled. "Sir, we..."

Kingston held his hand up. "It took me two minutes to get out of Sam what y'all should have found as soon as this accident happened. Thank me later."

He turned to walk away.

"Where are you going?" Officer Marsha asked, looking like she was about to follow.

Kingston turned back. "I flew all the way over here to see my niece. That's where I'm going."

Kingston resumed walking, then looked back to see Officer's Marsha and Robert still talking to Sam when he got to the corner.

"Gotta be another exit somewhere," he said to himself under his breath.

Kingston texted Billy and Tiana to let them know that he was on his way to see Elizabeth. He would be back soon to collect their bags to take to Rene's house. The last thing he needed to hear was her mouth about them spending money on a hotel.

The more Sam had talked, the more Kingston wanted to finish the ass whipping that Billy started. Right now, Elizabeth had a lot of explaining to do if she thought that she could get away with hurting his family.

Billy

Billy was looking at Rene. Just seeing her lying in bed, covered in bruises, he tried to be strong, but this was his baby girl. His mind flashed to Sam. Sam's sorry ass was still out in the waiting area, when he should have been in this room with his wife. That put the final nail in the coffin for Sam's guilt to Billy. Taking her hands in his, he placed them on his face as he talked to her. He looked at her from head to toe. Billy couldn't hold the tears any longer; he just let them flow, laying his head on her heart as he cried.

Tiana cried too.

Tiana

Tiana moved closer to be near Rene to let her know that they were there, waiting for her wake up. She brought Genesis for her to visit. She and Billy kept talking to Rene. They knew she could hear them. It was a matter of time before she opened her eyes. Just looking at Rene in this condition made Tiana's blood boil.

Elizabeth

Rodney was taking his time changing Elizabeth's tires. Elizabeth was dressed, and so was Leah. She couldn't wait to hit the road before the heat come crashing down on her. She knew Shelby would be arrested any second and she would make bail and be out free in no time. Changing her mind about pressing charges, Elizabeth decided she didn't want to be bothered with paperwork and courts. All she knew was that it was time to leave.

"Alright Elizabeth; your tires are changed and fixed. I also fixed your brakes lines and gave it a tune up. Now you're safe to drive," Rodney commented, giving that suggestive look at her again.

Elizabeth winked and gave Rodney fifty bucks, then placed Leah in her car seat. She locked her house doors, making sure to leave a window open, then drove off. First stop bank, store, and then it was goodbye Colorado.

Kingston

Paying the Uber driver for his services, Kingston got out and walked up to Elizabeth's porch. There was a man standing there, staring at him. Kingston rang the doorbell, then opened the screen door to knock.

"Hey, she is not home. She just left," the man said as he was picking up his tools.

"Do you know where Elizabeth went?" Kingston asked.

"No, but it looks like she was on her way out of town. Her bags were packed."

Kingston reached into his wallet, giving Rodney a hundred dollars. When he got out of the car, he had seen a window was open. Why in the hell she would leave her house like that if she was going out of town? *She must be a criminal in training,* Kingston thought.

"Thanks for the information," Kingston said to Rodney.

Pretending to be walking down the street, Kingston walked two houses over, jumped the fences and was climbing through Elizabeth's open window. Once inside, he looked to make sure she wasn't hiding anywhere in the house. Going into the kitchen, he opened the door to the garage and turned on the light. He saw the Lexus parked there. Walking down the steps, Kingston took out his phone, taking pictures of the damages. His hands shook when he saw fresh blood on the rim of the bumper, as well as the broken headlight and a dent.

Turning on the GPS computer in the car which was left unlocked, he took pictures of the last route and location, which was a highway. The wheels turned as it clicked in Kingston's mind.

"I'll be damned. She really did try to kill Rene. This computer confirms it. This entire car is proof," Kingston said to himself.

Kingston then did a conference call with Sam and Billy to let them know that Elizabeth was the person who tried to kill Rene, sending them pictures of the car.

Elizabeth

"Oh, shit! I forgot I left my other wallet. I got to turn around and get it," Elizabeth shouted.

Making a U-turn to go back, Elizabeth pulled up on the side of the curb, then entered her house. She could hear someone in her garage. Going to the hall closet, she took out her .38, walking slowly and hoping that whoever it was didn't hear her. Kingston walked up the stairs.

"What the hell are you doing in my house?" Elizabeth asked.

She aimed her gun at Kingston, just as they recognized each other. Elizabeth didn't have time to try to figure out why he was in her house though. She had moves to make.

Kingston took a step forward, and Elizabeth opened fire. Kingston's head fell forward before he collapsed to the floor.

Elizabeth ran to get her wallet, then hopped back into her car with Leah and peeled off, leaving Kingston alone.

Kingston

Kingston dripped in and out of consciousness. The neighbors all came outside at once now that Elizabeth's house was a crime scene. Officer Marsha arrived and asked Kingston if he could tell her who shot him. He used all of his strength to talk.

"Elizabeth shot me and she tried to kill my niece Rene. The car is in the garage. When I catch that bitch, I will feed her ass to the lion's den," Kingston whispered.

To Be Continued...

Dear Reader,

I hope you enjoyed this twisted story. Rene's family is a handful, but Elizabeth might be giving them a run for their money.

I would love to hear your thoughts on this book in the form of a rating or review.

Want to connect with me personally? Join my reader's group on Facebook: Queen's Royal Love Book Group.

Until next time,

Richelle T

www.ingramcontent.com/pod-product-compliance
Lightning Source LLC
Chambersburg PA
CBHW071702090426
42738CB00009B/1635